AE Russell

A Study of a Man and a Nation

Darrell Figgis

NONSUCH

First published 1916

Nonsuch Publishing Limited
73 Lower Leeson Street
Dublin 2
Ireland
www.nonsuchireland.com

Copyright © in this edition 2006 Nonsuch Publishing Limited

National Library Cataloguing in Publication Data.
A catalogue record for this book is available from the National Library.

ISBN 1 84588 543 0

Typesetting and origination by Tempus Publishing Limited
Printed and bound in Great Britain

AE Russell

A Study of a Man and a Nation

Contents

CHAPTER 1

THE MAN IN HIS DAYS

Standish O'Grady, one fair Sunday in summer, returned home a puzzled and an arrested man. He brought with him the news that he had heard, on the sea-front at Bray, the bearded figure of a young man in a tweed suit addressing the human flood before him, evangelizing (if one may use that word) the ancient pagan gods of Ireland. It was a lone spectacle. The sight of other young men, lit by a later faith and loud with tunes that made up in clamour what they lacked in music, or others more brightly apparelled, with big drums and brass instruments twisted into the likeness of the serpents they fought, and slightly indecent in the matter of past reminiscence, would have been appropriate enough to the scene. They would not have arrested the least incurious. Besides that, they would have been gregarious:

they would have fortified themselves with bigness as they fortified themselves with loudness. This was quite another thing. Spectacularly it was lonely. Lifted into the imagination it was lonelier yet; and something tragic withal. Its inappropriateness was its occasion, but that very fact gave it a gesture strange and appealing, gave it a voice that was like a slender rune of music that had wandered out of its place. What did these people, with one half of their devotions over for the day, or with the height of their weekly holiday come, want to know of Earth, the mother of us all, the Dana of ancient reverence, on whose bosom they trod unheedingly, having first hidden it beneath asphalt, like fleas on some elephant's back, thinking nothing of the great life, the deep knowledge, the throb of power beneath them; or of the great Shining Ones that are houselled within her or that throng the heavenly places in hierarchy on hierarchy of brightness and beauty and power, dimly perceived and dimly reverenced under many an ancient name in days when reverence had not been withered by tawdry pleasure, a huckster's vulgar gain, or the desperate oath from slumdom? Were they not the heirs of civilization? Had they not religions cut and suited to their order — or the order of their masters? Who then was this strange, wild man, whom they would not hear, and whom some few of them may have recognized as a clerk at Pim's and a mere shop assistant accordingly? What to them was the shining Lugh? This man at least was no Lugh, they would have rashly agreed. What of Balor? Balor, if they had heard of him, was, like Lugh, a myth; and they did not know themselves to be held in his one-eyed spell. As for Manannan, whose lips so lazily caressed the shore, could they not push their skiffs out upon his waters, and make the rowlocks, if need were, strain in contempt of such a one? Besides the man, though young, was not shaven. Plainly a peculiar case.

Standish O'Grady's thoughts are not recorded. We do not know if he felt like Oisin, that he would rather be with Finn and Caoilte in hell than with Patrick's God who took so queer a delight in burning. Very likely he did. Very likely he felt his place was rather beside this lonely figure than with the driftage of which he formed a part. It needs no imagination, however, to conceive that he felt less as if he had seen a strange sight than as if he had looked upon a portent. For the voice of ancient Ireland was speaking through this man; and speaking in an Anglicized watering-place.

In truth, it was a portent; and if Standish O'Grady had been the wise man we know him to be, he would have prayed, even without committing himself to the religious fire which burned in the young man's soul, that the portent might be of happy omen. For the social doctrine which it lit, and of which it formed an inevitable part, gave it a shrewdness of application. This was no fantastic faith that was being declared. Nor was this man an esoteric mystic who had been led away by the real light he saw to a lack of proportion the more disproportionate by being insistent and propagandist. Life seen through the eyes of a man concerned for ideals, that is to say, through the eyes of a man to whom religion is quite other than a matter of formal belief, resolves itself into something very sane and clean. It is essential, and because essential always possible, dignity and splendour are not to be waived by reference to modern complexities. Idealists are often quick logicians: this idealist particularly was so: and it would not avail to commit the first of logical fallacies by begging the very issue that was at debate. To create a degrading complexity, and then to argue the complexity in defence of the degradation, was hardly a procedure that would at any time, then or now, have confused for the preacher of the Bray promenade the battle in which he was engaged. Man, the child of Dana, and man crushed by a vast and nightmare engine, were not for him two persons, but one and the same person. Earth did not differentiate, though it was pitifully, tragically true that where some of her children bowed themselves before her, others failed from her. Therefore would he not differentiate? And so a social doctrine emerged in these Bray discourses that was shrewd in its simplicity, and worldly-wise because earthly-wise in its arraignment of a life that had fallen from greatness.

It was not from books that this came: certainly not from the writings of men who in those years prostrated themselves before the accomplished fact of degradation and saw in it the fine flower of civilization. As Æ confesses, between the ages of eighteen and thirty he hardly so much as read a newspaper; though that the affairs of his country did not pass unheeded many of his writings at that time show very clearly. His life was one of mystical experiment and experience; of study over the writings of ancient seers and initiates into the mysteries of the heavens and the earth, and over a wisdom once dearly cherished but now almost relinquished for the passions of the body and the irritations of the intellect; of contemplation and meditation; of a very rare circle of friendship that became finally, before its members were scattered through the world, almost a community of mind; and of a larger circle that acknowledged his leadership — we may hope, not too obsequiously — that turned to him for counsel, and accepted, it would appear, almost a spiritual dictatorship.

It is, or at least it should be, a whimsical humour with men who thereafter become more widely known when the private hazards of their life are greeted with attention. It must be a terrible moment in a man's life when he begins to live in the light of a coming biography — just as it is sometimes rather terrible for a reader when he begins to write letters for a coming collection of them. There is, however, none of the glance aside into a personal domestic rectitude that makes one vaguely uncomfortable when poets write of white flowers of blameless lives, in these days and private hours apart. That is just their significance. The best, because the deepest part of them, not only may not be searched, but cannot be told: because it is forbidden: because, even if it were not forbidden, there would be no words to tell them, since the only communication of them could be in the like experiences. They may only be known in their result. Four men who lived so rich, again because so experiential, a life together that they grew to something like a community of personality, where each was the fuller because of the others, each giving each his individual and essential quality, where yet none could have a strictly privy life because the community attained was so complete that their interchanges could dispense with words — this plainly is a matter that challenges to be divulged. And when it is remembered that the experiences and experiments that formed the groundwork of this community were mystical wisdom, discovered anew or housed in ancient writings, clearly the matter must be left to rest very tenderly as it was, though others who had to fight a somewhat lonely hand might covet the tale that would be told.

The only light we are suffered, other than that the mind engenders by brooding on the relation, is given in an incident related in a magazine to which they all, in the circle of which they formed a part, contributed. It was not told "because it is extraordinary," but "because it was a revelation of the secret of power, a secret which the wise in good and the wise in evil alike have knowledge of"; and it is told, as we divine, of one of that community who had come to a crisis in his spiritual life in which "two paths were open before him." "On one side lay the dazzling mystery of passion; on the other 'the small old path' held out its secret and spiritual allurements. I had hope," he says, that his friend "would choose the latter, and as I was keenly interested in his decision, I invested the struggle going on in his mind with something of universal significance, seeing in it a symbol of the strife between 'light and darkness, which are the world's eternal ways.' He came in late one evening. I saw at once by the dim light that there was something strange in his manner. I spoke to him in enquiry; he answered me in a harsh, dry voice quite foreign to his usual manner. 'Oh, I am not going to trouble myself any more, I will let things take their course.'....I soon saw what had happened; his mind, in which forces so evenly balanced, had fought so strenuously, had become utterly wearied out and could

work no longer. A flash of old intuition illumined it at last
— it was not wise to strive with such bitterness over life
— therefore he said to me in memory of this intuition, 'I
am going to let things take their course.' A larger tribunal
would decide; he had appealed unto Caesar. I sent him up
to his room and tried to quiet his fever by magnetization
with some success. He fell asleep, and as I was rather weary
myself I retired soon after."

To sleep came vision. In a "space opened on every side
with pale, clear light," "a slight wavering figure caught my
eye, a figure that swayed to and fro; I was struck with its
utter feebleness, yet I understood it was its own will or
some quality of its nature which determined that palpitat-
ing movement towards the poles between which it swung."
Above this figure "two figures, awful in their power, opposed
each other; the frail being wavering between them could
by putting out its arms, have touched them both. It alone
wavered, for they were silent, resolute, and knit in the conflict of will; they stirred not a hand nor a foot; there was
only a still quivering now and then as of intense effort, but
they made no other movement. Their heads were bent forward slightly, their arms folded, their bodies straight, rigid,
and inclined slightly backwards from each other like two
spokes of a gigantic wheel." These two "were the culmina-
tions of the human; towering images of the good and evil
man may aspire to. I looked at the face of the evil adept.
His bright red-brown eyes burned with a strange radiance
of power; I felt an answering emotion of pride, of personal intoxication, of psychic richness, rise up within me,
gazing on him. His face was archetypal; the abstract passion

which eluded me in the features of many people I knew, was here declared, exultant, defiant, gigantesque; it seemed to leap like fire, to be free. In this face, I was close to the legendary past, to the hopeless worlds where men were martyred by stony kings, where prayer was hopeless, where pity was none. I traced a resemblance to many of the great Destroyers in history whose features have been preserved — Napoleon, Rameses, and a hundred others, named and nameless, the long line of those who were crowned and sceptered in cruelty. His strength was in human weakness — I saw this, for space and the hearts of men were bare before me. Out of space there flowed to him a stream half invisible of red; it nourished that rich, radiant energy of passion; it flowed from men as they walked and brooded in loneliness, or as they tossed in sleep."

From this figure he turned to the other. "An aura of pale soft blue was around this figure, through which gleamed an underlight as of universal gold....I caught a glimpse of a face godlike in its calm, terrible in the beauty of a life we know only in dreams, with strength which is the end of the hero's toil, which belongs to the many times martyred soul....I understood how easy it would have been for this one to have ended the conflict, to have gained a material victory by its power, but this would not have touched on or furthered its spiritual ends. Only its real being had force to attract that real being which was shrouded in the wavering figure. This truth the adept of darkness knew also, and therefore he intensified within the sense of pride and passionate personality. Therefore they stirred not a hand nor a foot while under the stimulus of their presence, culminated the good and evil in the life which had appealed to a higher tribunal to decide. Then this figure, wavering between the two, moved forward and touched with its hand the Son of Light. All at once the scene and actors vanished, and the eye that saw them was closed; I was alone with darkness and a hurricane of thoughts."

Dreams are sometimes the body's torment; more happily they are the spirit's liberation; and here in dream one friend saw the issue that befell another in the deep world whence Life takes its rise, for the after-days revealed the fact that the conflict had been so decided. It tells little, yet a little, of what lay behind in the friendship it revealed; and it was only told, as it is told at some length here, because of the help it might give to others in like issue, for "although the gods and cosmic powers may war over us for ever, it is we alone declare them victors or vanquished"; but in it we may also see not a little of the conflicts of the inner life of those days, in the nest of that friendship and in the spiritual history of the man who was to emerge to more public hours.

The mind distantly perceives that such a community, once it was attained, would have to be broken before stagnation, or uniformity which is the same thing, should succeed; and when that happened one of that community was left in Ireland because his life belonged to Ireland, where one feels that the others did not. Born in Lurgan, in the County Armagh, on the 10th April, 1867, he came to the city of Dublin when he was about seven or eight years of age. He was put to school with one Doctor Benson in Rathmines, whose title to fame is this, and the fact that at the same time a fellow student was one who thereafter became known as Father George Tyrrell, of whom, however, Æ has no memory. It has never yet been satisfactorily decided why men are sent to school, though it is accounted a virtue in biography to discover the remarkable in that noisy comradeship. Except in certain modern instances, that happily invert the old procedure, and seek to educe rather than to cram, to differentiate rather than to demand conformity, and to help the divine in man to create the man by deftly providing it with chances for the display of itself rather than to contrive a series of formal qualifications, schooldom is a dull business, and the thing that shines out before and after is mysteriously extinguished (though not completely extinguished, as schoolmasters will be apt to complain) within its curriculum. Life triumphs in spite of rather than by reason of schooldom; and it is when, at the age of sixteen, Æ passed to the School of Art, where some degree of experiment was possible, that tuition may be said to begin.

It was here that he met W.B. Yeats, who was then prolific of verse, not having arrived at the caution of later years, and who, as a page of reminiscence recalls, "had a tendency to chant his verses to all in heaven and earth." A friendship was formed, based on Æ's part on sincere admiration. Both were Art students; and it was Æ's desire then to follow that gleam. The Master of Life (who must not, however, be weighted with all the decrees of livelihood) had another decision. Æ took his taste of what gentility has decided to call, in the case of those whom it afterwards decides to honour, economic pressure; and the following year found him in Pim's, a drapery house of the city.

The profoundest parts of a life are not its deeds but the long and slow preparations of personality necessary to those deeds; and these are untellable. Partly they are so because to seek to expound in round terms what were originally compounded of adventures, hesitancies, much incertitude and a slow dawning of light, mixed pitifully with bright illuminations and blackest despair, is to turn the facts of living into the lie of print; but partly also by what is implied in the modern making of books. Publicity has become a prohibition. Books are not published, as proclamations are supposed to be, for those whom it may concern, but for every curious eye to greet; and the result, however honesty may deplore it, has been a tighter drawing of the curtains about the secrets of the soul. If it were possible, as of old, to pass books about, like manuscripts, for those to read whom they would advance in the spiritual understanding which it is the essential function of a book to promote, what truer declarations of soul would result! What increased honesty, when honesty was a hand outstretched to one yet in the waters by one who had found a place for his feet!

Many perplexed literary matters would also become answered. One thinks of the publication, as a case in point, of the Browning Love Letters, that we would not willingly be without, despite the cheap journalist copy they have made. And when we face the next dozen odd years of Æ's life, the question arises sharply. Thousands work in drapers' shops at differing tasks with the same maddening uniformity, and pass to their evening pleasures (called, with a grim enough irony, re-creations), the dim corners of their private lives, expecting the one day of liberty, happily unknowing that the six days of bondage are already deflowering that liberty in advance, and who is to tell the ruin or painful achievement, the hopeful reachings-forward, the bitter relinquishments, each has in his own lonely world apart amid all the seeming dull and cheapened satisfaction? That is so when there is no ray of light to fall on any one soul of all the passing stream; but in the case of Æ the curiosity is sharpened by the fact that it was in those years that the man was formed and made.

Dublin is a human and humane city. Though an ominous Castle be in it, it is yet Irish in the preservation of homeliness, spontaneity, and the carelessness with which life should be worn if it is to have the grace proper to its dignity. Not only are friendships possible in it as (Dubliners would fain believe) they are not possible in less humane cities, but it is in itself, as a city, friendly. It caresses. It laughs. It is lit with understanding. It has a dignity that is easy, and in which all, save those that cluster about the ominous Castle, share with an accepted comradeliness. The result that we now know as Æ would not have been possible in any other city. Nor, it is worthy of remark, would it have been possible in a company that did not regard that edifice, and all it signified, with aversion, if not with the hostility with which a body reacts against a sore set in its midst.

Moreover — if indeed it be not part of the same large grace — hills are set about the city that are magical, although for the most part they refrain from austerity. They had their part in the making of the city's grace, for we may thank God that few parts of Ireland are, in physical distance or emotional kinship, far from Earth;

and they had also their separate part in the making of the man. It was about the time that the lad went first to drapery that he went first also to the Dublin hills. Until that time he lived in the city, and the hills were only a guardian company in mists of blue through some vista of the streets. And even when he went at last to the hills, it was with other boys to play, long before they unveiled themselves to him. Earth that cradles her brood of men nourishes them even when they do not recognize her; for it was not till he was sixteen or seventeen years of age, at a time when the body is tortured with desires that darken all the ways of life and make of the mind a torment of shame, that illumination first came to him, bringing with it the quickening of spiritual life.

It came quite spontaneously, without any definite prompting, for there were at that time no friendships capable in themselves of awakening it; and he took more continually to the company of the hills, while in his mind the new spiritual life warred with the old living. And when that occurs, the mind itself, the field of the issue, is in perplexity to know which life is more truly his, the new or the old, or which spirit is more truly owner of himself.

Thus, the illumination came, actually while on a visit to Armagh, and opened the new life that was to run beside the old to mock it by its contrast. It brought with it its own problems; for such new life comes like a strange thing inhabiting the blood. Nevertheless, illumination is illumination, for all its problems. For the world became transfigured; and, although dark days might come with the new torment of a lost glory, with the new torment of an old dead bodily life, Earth stood before him in an infinitely tender and living relation. It was about that time that he sang of her in a song of his earliest verse:

> She is rapt in dreams divine.
> As her clouds of beauty pass
> On our glowing hearts they shine,
> Mirrored there as in a glass.
>
> Earth, whose dreams are we and they,
> With her deep heart's gladness fills
> All our human lips can say
> Or the dawn-fired singer trills.

So he came to the conviction that the Youth of the World and the Age of Gold are not a past glory, but that it is only men — revolting perhaps from what they stupidly condemn as paganism — who have blinded themselves to a glory that ever remains new and young; and that conviction coming on illumination underlies all his thought and work. Unfortunately, such a vision gives an added stress to other things not at all so golden. Lit, thus, with a vision that gives a purpose to life, that arrays it like a battle while filling its hours with rich understanding; forming very rare friendships, the fitter because they gathered about that purpose and deepened it by enquiry and spiritual experiment; becoming, as time proceeded, the leader, and even dictator, to a wider circle that searched into the mysteries of the unveiled Earth (always a pleasing thing, even to the purest of heart); and learning to utter in song and prose, and limning by brush in colour and outline, the things which his spirit beheld in that world of enquiry: Æ was fortunate beside many another who had a lonelier track to take. Moreover, was there not among rare things that rarest: a city humane and friendly when it is the first law of cities to be inhuman and callous, and engirdled and guarded by wise hills, easy to be seen through some vista of the streets, in a world where the very fact of a city signifies a collective fear of the brown-visaged and beautiful mother? Surely he was fortunate. Yet it needs but a little sympathy — and, let it be said, experience, without which sympathy is a groping in darkness — to discover the darker thread in his days.

In the warp and woof that go to make the pattern of manhood in the loom of the years, it is the darker threads, happily or unhappily, that can least be guessed at. The life had its tragedy: in the truest sense, since there can be no tragedy where there is no splendour, missed or defeated: and there is a poem of that title to mark it:

> A man went forth one day at eve:
> The long day's toil for him was done:
> The eye that scanned the page could leave
> Its task until tomorrow's sun.

> Upon the threshold where he stood
> Flared on his tired eyes the sight,
> Where host on host the multitude
> Burned fiercely in the dusky night.

AE Russell: A Study of a Man and a Nation

The starry lights at play — at play —
The giant children of the blue,
Heaped scorn upon his trembling clay
And with their laughter pierced him through.

They seemed to say in scorn of him,
"The power we have was once in thee.
King, is thy spirit grown so dim,
That thou art slave and we are free?"

As out of him the power — the power —
The free — the fearless, whirled in play,
He knew himself that bitter hour
The close, of all his royal day.

And from the stars' exultant dance
Within the fiery furnace glow,
Exile of all the vast expanse,
He turned him homeward sick and slow.

Many have known that bitter hour; and many have pain-
fully relinquished a light that civilization, proud of its elaborate exploits and belauded by darkened minds, has not
suffered to let live, though older and simpler hours, labelled
in contempt by the queer terms of modern bookmaking
as barbaric, desired to preserve it. Many have known the
spirit of "Weariness," and have asked:

Where are now the dreams divine,
Fires that lit the dawning soul?

The Man in His Days

And have complained:

> I think
> Old companions of the prime
> From our garments well might shrink,
> Muddied with the lees of Time.
>
> Fade the heaven-assailing moods:
> Slave to petty tasks I pine
> For the quiet of the woods,
> And the sunlight seems divine.
>
> And I yearn to lay my head
> "Where the grass is green and sweet;
> Mother, all the dreams are fled
> From the tired child at thy feet.

There is a settled hopelessness in these poems that tell of the man in the midst of the "petty tasks" to which he was a daily slave. They were born of utter weariness, of fagged and defeated energies, when the will will hardly be persuaded that the light once gone can ever return. There is a louder revolt in "A Return":

> We turned back mad: we thought of the morrow,
> The iron clang of the far-away town;
> We could not weep in our bitter sorrow,
> But joy as the Arctic sun went down.

That tells the tale of a concluded holiday (the attentive ear, to whom these things are not the chance of a poem, will notice the plural instead of the singular pronoun!); but in each there is something nearer to tragedy than in the in-and-out of kings, for it concerns a kingship less accidental and nearer sympathy. At worst an idle interest, at best a distant rumour, to those who have not lived through such hours, to those who know, and the world is of such, such poems will be of special significance in the life of a man who was to emerge to days when work was work indeed, however fatiguing, and not a dull monotonous labour. Acquainted with what is called "economic stress," but for which a wit has presented them with the apter word "wagery", they will know the value of the anvil and the hammer in the making of the man because both anvil and hammer are so very familiar.

CHAPTER II

DISCOVERIES

During these years manhood and the man were in the making. The purpose of his days, without the discovery of which a man's life is as spilled water, became clearer to him. The rhythms that swing through darkness and brightness carry a man onward to a finer certitude if the will is not unbent like a tired archer's bow; and there is a despair, though it seem hopeless when it comes, that is more full of hope than contentment. It is by his aspirations, not by his achievements, that a man is to be measured.

We know very well, in spite of so much that lies hidden in the involutions of living, what these years meant for Æ. We have not only the more mature result. We have his discoveries by the way. It is the common thought that poets write to declare their visions to others; and this is in some measure true, in that songs would not be sung were there not an audience to attend, and visions would not be declared were there not the hope that there were some whom it would concern; yet at heart the poet finds that he sings to declare his vision to himself, to expound and complete it for himself, to record for himself his discoveries in the spiritual thrift of his soul. With the higher company of poets, with those whom in glib phrase we undertake to call major poets, this is so. In English poetry where Herrick made songs, Shelley made discoveries, and therefore, where Herrick bettered his art Shelley bettered his vision. In the defter use of words of one we do not see a deeper vision, whereas with Shelley the greater clarity of his music inevitably, as the mind perceives, flowed down from the purer heights to which he had ascended. To pass from the poems he wrote when he thought himself an atheist at Oxford, to the great chorus in "Hellas", is not to read a volume of poetry, it is to pass through a spiritual history. So it was with Whitman, with Beethoven, with Michelangelo, with Æschylus, in their several arts, and with all of those whom the world in calling artists recognizes as the recorders of spiritual aspiration, the creators of great and pure decisions of the soul.

There is therefore a slight grudge against Æ when in his *Collected Poems* he dispersed the order which in conversation he always recognizes. To think of life as an ideal splendour is only in a coward's shrift to release it from the details of living. If there were times when the accountant from Pim's came out upon the threshold of the building for the stars of heaven to mock his tired brain with the taunt of a kingship grown so dim, as "he turned him homeward sick and slow," it was also true that there were times when the accountant's desk was whirled away while distant sights with strange people in unfamiliar surroundings came clearly before the eye. Poems such as "Om," "Oversoul," and "The Earth Breath," are records of such experiences; and from the sight the poet gives us of the man who went forth one day at eve, for the just balance of those days we may turn to the sight the poet, seated at his desk, himself had, where:

> the restless ploughman pauses,
> Turns and, wondering,
> Deep within his rustic habit
> Finds himself a king;
> For a fiery moment looking
> With the eyes of God
> Over fields a slave at morning
> Bowed him to the sod.

His first volume, "Homeward, Songs by the Way," published in 1894, and many of the poems in "The Earth Breath," published three years later, were the fruit of this time. They pretended to be no more than a garner of spiritual experiences, a portion of his life from one who regarded this public canvassing of his inmost life with aversion. Such an aversion is not a singular fact in authorship. It may, paradox though it be, like the heart of man, be said to be the ruling fact of authorship; for none like to display their holy or their unholy things before a throng; and the very lewdest of honesty is not exempt from that. It is right, for instance, to conceive of Hazlitt putting out his "Liber Amoris" with a gesture of shuddering. Authorship is not the trite affair the modern trade of writing has made it to seem. With Æ, however, the facts were singular. All the poems had appeared already in the *Irish Theosophist*, a magazine that was privately printed by the circle into which Æ had drifted when the "divine visitations" led him to seek out companionship in spiritual enquiry; and it was to this circle he put his case, and it was they who decided that the poems should be published. He had become the leader of this circle; and he was the main scribe for the monthly magazine they printed, writing from various points of view in a variety of deliberately conceived styles under different pen-names. Wanting at one time a new pen-name, he subscribed himself as ÆON. His penmanship not at all times being of the legiblest, the printer deciphered the first diphthong and set a query for the rest; whereupon the writer, in his proof-sheets, stroked out the query and stood by the diphthong. And to mark the detachment with which "Homeward, Songs by the Way" was to be published, an escape was made into this pen-name, though the authorship was at no time a secret.

For some years W.B. Yeats had lived in London, engaging in literary journalism. Already he had established himself as a poet of very rare beauty; and his choice of subject, a certain atmosphere laden with mist that wrapped the beauty (for which he himself "coined the funny nickname" "The Celtic Twilight"), and the fact that he travelled to and fro between Ireland and England, caused the right ascription of his poetry to this country, though it was framed in the English tongue. He and Æ were close friends. He knew the circle that met in Ely Place. He even once for a short while joined the "household" that lived in Ely Place, sharing the life of spiritual experiment. Admiring Æ as he was in turn admired by Æ, and conceivably not being averse to another text in his own special subject in London journalism (for to succeed in London journalism, then as now, was to make a special corner, with a certain allowance for versatility), it came about therefore, with the publication of "Homeward, Songs by the Way," that he and Æ were hailed as the leaders of a queer thing known as the Irish Literary Revival. It was queer in this, that neither of them knew Irish; but they came at a time when Englishmen had the inward conviction, hardly to be publicly admitted, that their language had exhausted its chances of beautiful usage, and was only of avail thenceforward for journalism. There was, to be sure, some justification for this suspicion, for poets and prose-men had become afraid of beauty; they regarded fine writing askance (and do yet); they defied new forms that should give greater suppleness, and had long and bitterly fought the greatest living master of their language; and it was therefore not altogether a strange thing that the best of its music at the time was won by those who used the tongue as foreigners, these two Irishmen in verse and Joseph Conrad, a Pole, in prose. Even the very great poem that succeeded to them from the pen of an Englishman, "The Dynasts," was cast into a verse that simulated prose; and was a feat of imagination rather in the greatness of its conception than in the making of its verses, being fearful of the metaphor in which the elder poets delighted, and tucking its legerdemain into stage-directions.

What was called the "Irish Literary Revival" was truly an English Literary Revival conducted by Irishmen. In this W.B. Yeats had a conscious part; but Æ was rather caught into it from his own separate world, that was only literary in the sense that to convey spiritual experiences from soul to soul was to put them into writing, and that to convey them justly was to write them finely, with a commensurate music and imagination. W.B. Yeats' apostleship was designed and deliberate, and the immediate results were excellent though the work became spoiled in time; but Æ was rather an unsuspecting apostle, a little bewildered in the white light of publicity that had so suddenly fallen about him in his emergence from the household in Ely Place. The difference may be seen in their work. In Yeats' poetry there is the same deliberate disavowal of splendour that marked the work of his peers in London; and it arose from the same literary fear of the past — a fear that if splendour were permitted it would slip into the grooves cut by the prowess of the elder poets. Francis Thompson might have reassured them; but the critics took good care that he should not by at once likening him, in much dreary nonsense, to Crashaw, and deriving him from the Restoration poets, till one wonders if they had bothered to read Thompson's fiery page of metaphors or had turned down Crashaw's taut music from its lumber on the shelves. However, for the most part the critics were the poets and the poets were the critics, and in this literary genealogy-hunting they showed their own fear of the past. In this fear Yeats shared; but, coming to it from the County Sligo and the city of Dublin, and with the soul of a poet born not made, he made beautiful poetry where

Discoveries

Ernest Dowson (save for one solitary cry of passion) played with trivialities, where Lionel Johnson wrought scholarly verse, and Hobert Bridges relied for the most part on bald statement. He made a convention as they did. "The Celtic Twilight" was a literary convention, conceived in London and conceivably revolting from London; for the old Gaelic poets were not afraid of splendour, of metaphor, of big musics; indeed, they rioted in them; they splashed in them as a swimmer glad of the sea, laughing back to the bright laughter of the wave. Yet conventions are a little thing, for he made poetry; and "The Countess Cathleen," wrought in those days, justifies nothing, and asks to justify nothing, but itself, for Beauty needs no creed for its making or its defence.

Æ, however, was not even aware of the stones on which W.B. Yeats had sharpened his literary tools. His nights were spent in psychic experiment or in brooding over the "Bhagavad Gita", the "Upanishads", and song-offerings and ancient wisdom hid of old in the secret house of books; and thus, along these lines, with no mere literary interest, coming to the old gods which the race once saw peopling the hills of Ireland. He had no fear for echoes from the past, if echoes from the past gave him what he wanted. His "Symbolism" was not a fantastic Parisian creed, but something much simpler and direct.

> Now when the spirit in us wakes and broods,
> Filled with home yearnings, drowsily it flings
> From its deep heart high dreams and mystic moods,
> Mixed with the memory of the loved earth things:

Clothing the vast with a familiar face;
Reaching its right hand forth to greet the starry race.

He lost as he gained: he was more content to record his discovery than to communicate it: had he as a poet been more self-aware he might by a better craft, born of brooding, have more often lit a flame in his verse, to burn intensely there and to light other brains, where it is content to tell of a fire in the poet himself altogether so much brighter than in the poetry he made. There is no poem, so sincere is this poet, and especially in his early verse, that does not tell of a vision that he does not feel that it is important we should know. He was never at heart interested in the poem only for the poem's sake; and he never in his verse took a holiday — at least in his published verse. And we feel this. We feel that there is no poem, however it fail, that does not record a spiritual discovery; but we are often baffled, because the poem, while it tells us of the discovery, is not itself the fine ritual in which the discovery is involved. The poet has his vision, we know; though visions are by no means always the starting-point for song, yet we are seldom uncertain in this case. Indeed, that is the thing that tantalizes. For the magician's sleight sometimes is lacking; and thus we hear him telling us of things, sometimes facilely and always mellifluously, but we are disappointed because he cannot make his vision ours forever. At such times, we feel that if he had brooded over his craft as he brooded over the things he wished to convey by his craft he would have made us better sharers of the things that remain his.

For the poems of these days are one continuous inspiration of theme. "Homeward, Songs by the Way" is an unbroken series. It is linked with "The Earth Breath" by the inclusion in that volume of many poems of the first song; the last of which appeared in "The Divine Vision," where the poet first begins definitely to turn to speechcraft from songcraft, and to utter in a fine pomp what he first had sung in purity, even though the song were not always uniformly magical.

These are hard things, not easy to understand, that the lover only will consider. The poet himself would fain believe that the vision uplifting him will bring its own song with it, that the beauty and splendour of the one will be the infallible beauty and splendour of the other. He will agree that the song may rush straight upon his lips from the thing seen, or that the certainty of a poem may come in some rare uplifting of the mind though that poem will lie buried for months, its shape and fashion all unknown, to flow forth finally with a deeper earthly wisdom, though with not so clear a light: he will agree that the vision itself, for all that it is, will not be clear to him till its poem come, and that he will make the vision his by the making of the poem, rising upon it by being now finished with it: but it will seem to him that these things should argue a poem to match equally with the exaltation given to him, and that if the poem be faulty there was something amiss with the exaltation. So, indeed, at heart it mostly is; but not always. All men are more than they can express of themselves. No man can give another all of his own enlightenment. And if a man passes rapidly on from one thing to another, content with equally rapid expressions, others will lose in the degree in which he gains — though it is equally true that he himself will also lose in the end. He thus becomes the converse of the man who stays at a few poems all his life, whittling at them till much of their early beauty is gone, he having passed away from the mood in which they came to him.

We feel this most in some of Æ's later poems, published in "The Divine Vision" in 1908; in his early poems the case is even more difficult. It is an impertinence to question the form in which a poem comes to us; it is doubly an impertinence from one poet to another, for poets should be, though they are not always, glad when a brother adds to the created beauty of the world — as this poet happily gives thanks for the gift of Æ's book of song. Yet a poem may be taken where the clearness of the vision is indisputable and the result one to be pondered on, where, however, the answering mood in us is not uplifted to an equal height. Such a poem is "Om". We know how it came. As the accountant sat at his desk, it and all around him were whirled away while he looked intently on the sight before his open eyes.

> Faint grew the yellow buds of light
> Far flickering beyond the snows,
> As leaning o'er the shadowy white
> Morn glimmered like a pale primrose.

> Within an Indian vale below
> A child said, "Om" with tender heart,

Discoveries

Watching, with loving eyes, the glow
In dayshine fade and night depart.

The word which Brahma at his dawn
Outbreathes and endeth at his night,
Whose tide of sound so rolling on
Gives birth to orbs of pearly light;

And beauty, wisdom, love, and youth,
By its enchantment gathered, grow
In agelong wandering to the truth,
Through many a cycle's ebb and flow.

And here the voice of earth was stilled,
The child was lifted to the Wise:
A strange delight his spirit filled
And Brahm looked from his shining eyes.

The record of the thing seen is complete, told with music
and wisdom. But what have we missed? We have missed
just what it brought to the poet. The ecstasy it wrought
in him he has not wrought in us, for all that we know
well, from the record and some alchemy in its making, that
the ecstasy was there. The very chord he heard is hardly
heard by us, for it is strange that the tone conveyed by the
word "Om" is not the tone-dominant of the poem. Pedants
may wrangle over some ill-befitting slender vowels, but
the fact remains, for we know that there are tones, and a
sequence in tones, could men but find them, that are more
meaningful, more profoundly significant, than all the poor

logical conveyances of words, upbuilding and creating souls and shattering unworthy moods, lifting the spirit through circles and circles of light. It is the poet's business to find these tones that shall express by their utterance, each in its own utterance, all that he would put into words; and when he finds them we hear the ecstasy. That is his high prophetic task, that the musician himself may envy him. When he has heard his tone, when the meaningful chord of its music sings through his soul, he has what we tritely call his divine afflatus. Patience, an intent and watchful calm, and care will give him the rest of the poem, as the tone rolls onward and concludes itself; and then the afflatus is communicated to us.

So hear this other, "The Great Breath," by contrast.

Its edges foamed with amethyst and rose,
Withers once more the old blue flower of day:
There where the ether like a diamond glows
Its petals fade away.

A shadowy tumult stirs the dusky air;
Sparkle the delicate dews, the distant snows;
The great deep thrills, for through it everywhere
The breath of Beauty blows.

I saw how all the trembling ages past,
Moulded to her by deep and deeper breath,
Neared to the hour when Beauty breathes her last
And knows herself in death.

We are told nothing here, but, despite the slight stumble at the opening of the last stanza, we are lifted to an equal mood; the ecstasy that was in the singer is the ecstasy that passes to us. So it is with "The Unknown God," with its higher, clearer tone, and "Refuge" from his later volume, with its deep mature reticence. Yet, whether we hear or do not hear his ecstasy, never was there so exact a poet as this. Many of his poems come not only from the inmost circle of spiritual insight, but also from the outer circle of psychic vision; and much that might seem, at a cursory glance, extravagant imagery, will be found to be no more than meticulous accuracy to what he has beheld. Perhaps they too much demand a knowledge of mystic signs and symbols; perhaps they unwisely, in some cases, decree for us a like psychic experience if not learning — unwisely for poetry, which should not need annotation but should address itself directly to the pure and aspiring spirit of man: that may very well be; but there are none of his poems that we may set aside as inexact. "The Robing of the King," for example, records precisely what in vision he beheld, rightly or wrongly, as the meaning of the Crucifixion, surrendering, as he does, its outward appearance to those who did not know the esoteric event that was happening. And there are many poems of this sort, that are rather less poems than texts, like the texts of the East, to be brooded upon like symbols and unravelled like mysteries. Not only, however, are the visions of the "household" so written. On the hills of Ireland, aflame once with mystic fires, this man may have beheld the great ones once again, have seen things not easy to be told, and have recorded them with the care of a man of faith. These things are not lightly to be spoken of; but to be passed from hand to hand; and Irishmen at least will read "The Child of Destiny" with attention.

For this poet conceived highly of Life, and conceived highly of Poetry, the first and purest handmaiden of Life. He never used Poetry for his own hand, or suborned it with his prejudices. He might lightly say of himself:

> He has built his monument
> With the winds of time at strife,
> Who could have before he went
> Written on the book of life;

But it is because he wrote first in the book of life that his book of poetry will be esteemed by the wise. What his thought of poetry was he declared when another poet, not so clean of heart, slandered his country. Irishmen are not, as a rule, among those who highly esteem Rudyard Kipling. His book of verse wakes few echoes in them. That he should insolently have traduced their dear land — he who has no land, but only a windy Empire wherein to wander — is perhaps a small matter; that he should have debauched song is a deeper trouble in a land where the poet was of old time honoured because the poet honoured his craft. And when this man laid foul words at Ireland's door in a simulation of poetry, taking Scripture as a text for his baseness, Æ replied in prose. As that reply is not elsewhere available, it shall be recorded here in full, as much of the man is in it.

Discoveries

I speak to you, brother, because you have spoken to me, or rather you have spoken for me. I am a native of Ulster. So far back as I can trace the faith of my forefathers they held the faith for whose free observance you are afraid.

I call you brother, for so far as I am known beyond the circle of my personal friends, it is as a poet. We are not a numerous tribe, but the world has held us in honour because on the whole in poetry is found the highest and sincerest utterance of man's spirit. In this manner of speaking if a man is not sincere his speech betrayeth him, for all true poetry was written on the Mount of Transfiguration, and there is revelation in it and the mingling of heaven and earth. I am jealous of the honour of poetry, and I am jealous of the good name of my country, and I am impelled by both emotions to speak to you.

You have Irish blood in you. I have heard, indeed, Ireland is your mother's land, and you may, perhaps, have some knowledge of Irish sentiment. You have offended against one of our noblest literary traditions in the manner in which you have published your thoughts. You begin by quoting Scripture. You preface your verses on Ulster by words from the mysterious oracles of humanity as if you had been inflamed and inspired by the prophet of God; and you go on to sing of faith in peril and patriotism betrayed and the danger of death and oppression by those who do murder by night, which things, if one truly feels, he speaks of without consideration of commerce or what it shall profit him to speak. But you, brother, have withheld your fears for your country and mine until they could yield you a profit in two continents. After all this high speech about the Lord and the hour of national darkness it shocks me to find this following your verses: "Copyrighted in the United States of America by Rudyard Kipling" You are not in want. You are the most successful man of letters of your time, and yet you are not above making profit out of the perils of your country. You ape the lordly speech of the prophets, and you conclude by warning everybody not to reprint your words at their peril. In Ireland every poet we honour has dedicated his genius to his country without gain, and has given without stint, without any niggardly withholding of his gift when his nation was in dark and evil days. Not one of our writers when deeply moved about Ireland has tried to sell the gift of the spirit... You, brother, hurt me when you declare your principles and declare a dividend to yourself out of your patriotism openly and at the same time.

I would not reason with you but that I know there is something truly great and noble in you, and there have been hours when the immortal in you secured your immortality in literature, when you ceased to see life with that hard cinematograph eye of yours and saw with the eyes of the spirit, and power and tenderness and insight were mixed in magical tales. Surely you were far from the innermost when, for the first time I think, you wrote of your mother's land and my countrymen.

I have lived all my life in Ireland holding a different faith from that held by the majority. I know Ireland as few Irishmen know it, county by county, for I travelled all over Ireland for years, and, Ulster man as I am, and proud of the Ulster people, I resent the crowning of Ulster with all the virtues and the dismissal of other Irishmen as thieves and robbers. I resent the cruelty with which you, a stranger, speak of the most lovable and kindly people I know.

You are not even accurate in your history when you speak of Ulster's traditions and the blood our forefathers spilt. Over a century ago, Ulster was the strong and fast place of rebellion, and it was in Ulster that the Volunteers stood beside their cannon and wrung the gift of political freedom for the Irish Parliament. You are blundering in your blame. You speak of Irish greed in I know not what connection, *unless you speak of the war waged over the land; and yet you ought to know that both parties in England have by Act after Act confessed the absolute justice and rightness of that agitation, Unionist no less than Liberal, and both boast of their share in answering the Irish appeal. They are both proud today of what they did. They made enquiry into wrong and redressed it.*

But you, it seems, can only feel sore and angry that intolerable conditions imposed by your laws were not borne in patience and silence. For what party do you speak? When an Irishman has a grievance you smite him. How differently would you have written of Runnymeade and the valiant men of England who rebelled whenever they thought fit. You would have made heroes out of them....

Have you no soul left, after admiring the rebels in your own history, to sympathize with other rebels suffering deeper wrongs? Can you not see deeper into the motives for rebellion than the hireling reporter who is sent to make up a case for the paper of a party? The best men in Ulster, the best Unionists in Ireland, will not be grateful to you for libelling their countrymen in your verse. For, let the truth be known, the mass of Irish Unionists are much more in love with Ireland than with England. They think Irish Nationalists are mistaken, and they fight with them, and they use hard words, and all the time they believe Irishmen of any party are better in the sight of God than Englishmen. They think Ireland is the best country in the world to live in, and they hate to hear Irish people spoken of as murderers and greedy scoundrels. Murderers! Why there is more murder done in any four English shires in a year than in the whole of the four provinces of Ireland. Greedy! The Nation never accepted a bribe, or took it as an equivalent or payment for an ideal, and what bribe would not have been offered to Ireland if it had been willing to forswear its traditions.

AE Russell: A Study of a Man and a Nation

*I am a person whose whole being goes into a blaze at the thought
of oppression of faith, and yet I think my Catholic countrymen
infinitely more tolerant than those who hold the faith I was born in.
I am a heretic judged by their standards, a heretic who has written
and made public his heresies, and I have never suffered in friendship
or found my heresies an obstacle in life. I set my knowledge, the
knowledge of a lifetime, against your ignorance, and I say you have
used your genius to do Ireland and its people a wrong. You have
intervened in a quarrel of which you do not know the merits like any
brawling bully who passes and only takes sides to use his strength.
If there was a high court of poetry, and, those in power jealous of
the noble name of poet and that none should use it save those who
were truly Knights of the Holy Ghost, they would hack the golden
spurs from your heels and turn you out of the Court. You had the
ear of the world and you poisoned it with prejudice and ignorance.
You had the power of song, and you have always used it on behalf
of the strong against the weak. You have smitten with all your might
at creatures who are frail on earth but mighty in the heavens, at
generosity, at truth, at justice, and Heaven has withheld vision and
power and beauty from you, for this your verse is only a shallow
newspaper article made to rhyme. Truly ought the golden spurs to be
hacked from your heels and you be thrust out of the Court.[1]*

More than once it has happened that a petty deed awoke a
memorable rebuke; and this rebuke is memorable because
of what it reveals of the austere faith of a poet who happens
also to be, whatever the rank of his poetry in the judgment of time, possibly the greatest writer, certainly one of
the very great writers, of English prose of his time. That
his prose dares to be eloquent, daring also to be gorgeous

without any of the trappings of prose feudaldom, is itself a rare excellence in a day when the writing of prose has come under the bondage of the journalist. That it has hitherto only been accessible in stray pamphlets and booklets, some of the best of it being even yet hidden in old numbers of mystical papers and early national journals, has obscured its united excellence. It is curious, and yet not strange, that three such writers of English prose as Æ, Standish O'Grady, and "John Eglinton", each so distinct, each eloquent though in such differing ways — the calm river of John Eglinton's prose, where the music ripples over smooth stones under the deceptive appearance of baldness, the pomp of Standish O'Grady's periods, like the brave chant of an ancient Gael, and Æ, rich with a subtle music, dealing with things hard to relate, full of colour and allusion and eloquence — should have been working together, John Eglinton touching Æ on the mystical side and Standish O'Grady arousing him to the bardic glory of the race and to its reverence for the hero-heart. But then Dublin, as has been said, is a friendly city. And these writers of prose have not yet won their due place where the makers of poetry have already passed from the first glory of estimation — a curious inversion of the usual treatment accorded to prose and poetry.

It always happens, if a man be a poet, that his prose will be an elaboration, in a differing, ritual of words, of the ideas which received their quintessential form in his poetry. Either that or his prose will be, as Milton haughtily said his was writ with his left hand. "I ask with Mitchell," says Æ,[2] "who was told of the laying of the Atlantic cable: 'Will a lie told at one end come out truth at the other?' The spiritual question is the only really important one." That is the poet looking out on life, fallen so far from the greatness it yet remembers. "Poets," says Shelley, "are the unacknowledged legislators of the world"; but Æ comes forward in his prose, as all poets in their measure do, and presses for the acknowledgment. It is a light thing that they should be acknowledged by this or that trivial honour, too often given not as an acknowledgment but as a deft and social grace with which to avoid the real case at issue. Rather, the poet, building his temple of beauty, each stone of which in its careful hewing is an implicit condemnation of the city without, and finding his temple neglected, as such temples are too often wont to be, or merely extolled in set terms from the distance, comes forth and addresses the city. As his building was, so will his address be, for it is his single-mindedness that brings him out. Would he not rather be at his building? But what use to build if the city, instead of remembering the Heavenly City which his temple was to recall, denies every line of his beauty (while perhaps giving it some light lip-fealty) by erecting monstrous structures without as it sings some queer and unintelligible chant about progress? Even if he does not fall into the quite false logic of thinking that his building in such a case would be mere selfishness, he will at least rightly ask himself if it is not high time he challenged his fellow-citizens as to the first principles of their buildings and of his. He will know that he holds the logic of the position, for they give a certain kind of fealty to his building, whereas he gives none to theirs.

Later on Æ was called upon to go out and give a hand in the building of the city itself, when his prose took a

workaday directness. Tracts on pig-breeding, and journalism that had to deal with any subjects that might chance to
come within his reach and insist, patiently or impatiently,
on certain essential things week-in and week-out, are not
that portion of a man's endeavours that he hopes to pass as a
cherished possession to a wider and a later world; but there
are other parts of his later work as a nation-builder where
a simple and direct economy was demanded of him; which
he gave; giving it eloquence moreover, such as bestows on
it other qualities than that of shrewd sense, and makes it
memorable for reasons deeper than that of logic. For his
audience then was not elect: it was desirable that the simple
should hear him; it was inevitable that knavery would hear
him, and seek to pervert his words, to represent him as a
mere fool of a poet or, alternatively, as deeper knave even
than they, with an even craftier design on the pockets of the
simple. Before that time, however, his audience was elect.
They were the few who had gathered about the temple,
were even within the temple, with some very few who
had helped to hew its stones; and to these he could speak
all of his mind.

It is usually faulty thinking to speak of one style being
simpler than another. Pedantries there are; but in the main
the difference between one style and another is in the
matter that it contains, and the circumstances attending
its presentation. To say of Æ's later style that it is simple
is really only to say that he stated in it the results of his
thinking in final and orderly terms. All of his mind was
not in it; only its last conclusions: not the visions, not
the spiritual convictions that the visions brought, not the

outlook on life, the fine inspiration, the intense uplifting, linked with those convictions, not the delicate perceptions between this and that uplifting, this and that Beauty, this and that Truth, between inspiration and aspiration, not the processes leading outward from the experiences of a man of such an involution of spiritual life to his conclusions of the kind of world in which the greatness which is in man would best thrive: nothing of all this; but just those last conclusions, put together with a certain show of reason and a certain logical structure. The other things belong to the fine intimacies of spiritual life, whereas the conclusions deal only with the apt environment for that spiritual life. If a man has to write, however, of those fine intimacies the writing will be just as complex as the spiritual life is complex, and will seem obscure in exactly the same relation as his experiences and discoveries will defy expression. He will have to ambush the shy things that lurk in the thicket of his soul, and net them subtly and quickly in the tones and colours and rhythms of words rather than in their bold and limited meanings. That will not lead to clarity; clarity in such a case would be a profound lie; for precious things are precious in both meanings of the word.

It is a very delicate net of words, for instance, he has thrown round some of the intimations of the spiritual meaning of Life in his essay "The Renewal of Youth". "We came out of the Great Mother-Life for the purposes of soul," he says; and in the wonderful music of that essay he writes of the source and destiny of that experience for which we have been lent to Life.

In some moment of more complete imagination, the thought-born may go forth and look on the ancient Beauty. So it was in the mysteries long ago and may well be today. The poor dead shadow was laid to sleep, forgotten in its darkness, as the fiery power, mounting from heart to head, went forth in radiance. Not then did it rest, nor ought we. The dim worlds dropped behind it, the lights of earth disappeared as it neared the heights of the immortals. There was One seated on a throne, One dark and bright with ethereal glory. It arose in greeting. The radiant figure laid its head against the breast which grew suddenly golden, and Father and Son vanished in that which has no place or name.

That of which he writes is the same, we divine, as he sang of in "The Robing of the King"; and to say of it, as of the essay, that it is prose at its highest, is to give it but half its praise. It is the writing of a seër: a seër who sees the golden end with the golden uprise, and who perceives, therefore, that "every word which really inspires is spoken as if the Golden Age had never passed," for "the great teachers ignore the personal identity and speak to the eternal pilgrim." It may be true, in the opening words of this essay, that "humanity is no longer the child it was at the beginning of the world," that "its gay, wonderful childhood gave way, as cycle after cycle coiled itself into slumber, to more definite purposes, and now it is old and burdened with experiences" — experiences gathered, as his profound faith is, not merely as written in histories dealing with the outward life of nations and the race, but in renewed reincarnations of innumerable souls — but it is equally true that the life that runs now is the life that ever ran; and if we could but strike down to that depth, or if some seër could do so, or if some artist, who is the seër expressing himself in Beauty, could do so, then we would renew our youth, we would smile in the face of old Circumstance with the youngling joy that is our true heritage, and like happy children wise with understanding refashion Seeming into the ideal truth of Being. The true poems, says Whitman, whom he quotes with approbation—

> Bring none to his or to her terminus or to be content and full,
> Whom they take, they take into space to behold the birth of
> stars, to learn one of the meanings,
> To launch off with absolute faith, to sweep through the ceaseless
> rings and never be quiet again.

Therefore he says of himself: "I am one of those who would bring back the old reverence for the Mother, the magic, the love"; for it is to the Mother we go, to lay our head there, and learn again the secrets of ourselves — and to the Father too, the bright and lonely Spirit from whom all things emerge, though he does not speak of this here.

"The Renewal of Youth" is great prose, quite conceivably the greatest prose of its time; but it is this firstly because it is, in strict terms, a holy book. It is not concerned with dead things, with ethics and moralities, but with the fount from which these things arise, and in connection with which they are not dead but alive. "Our companion struggles in some labyrinth of passion. We help him, we think, with ethics and moralities. Ah, very well they are; well to know and to keep, but wherefore? For their own sake? No, but that the King may arise in his beauty....Let a man but feel for what high cause is his battle, for what is his cyclic labour, and a warrior who is invincible fight for him and he draws upon divine powers." Life looked at as the writer of this book regards it, is a great and holy thing. Mysticism, is it? Then not mysticism as modernly conceived: a thing of study rather than of experience. "The soul of the modern mystic," as he himself says in this very essay, "is becoming a mere hoarding-place for uncomely theories. He creates an uncouth symbolism, and obscures his soul within with names drawn from the Kabala or ancient Sanskrit, and makes alien to himself the intimate powers of his spirit, things which in truth are more his than the beatings of his heart"; and any one who has had knowledge of the charlatanry of much of modern Theosophy will know how true this is, and why Æ shrinks at the use of that word. Setting aside names of sects and movements that obscure because they label living things, the vision seen here is a thing of spiritual experience, which, because it is spiritual and therefore central, defines all the parts of life as they present themselves to view.

In his other essays that definition is seen, or that experience further expounded. "The Renewal of Youth" itself is woven together from articles in the *Irish Theosophist*. In that magazine he wrote under many pen-names; but apart from his own initials or the signature of "Æ" there is only one other token that at all comes near the central outlook of the man. Many of these essays have not been published, or gathered up in the sweep of other work. Some of them, indeed, as is inevitable in all work that remains occasional though it be writ with a burning purpose, must rest where it is. The writer will hardly disentangle it from a hurried mood, or rescue it from an hour that could not wait for the complete maturing of a thought. Some of it, both from this magazine and the *Internationalist* that succeeded to it, has already been recovered. Others not less valuable remain yet unpublished. And in all of them the thought of the man — or, since words decline from their former meanings, less the thought than the vision of the man — shines clearly, viewing the circumstances of Life from the certitudes to which he has attained.

Life for him having flowed from the great life of the Mother, rolling through ages when the sources of that life were more clearly known and when therefore the sources of power, of splendour, of simple dignity were more purely taught by the wise, he is desirous of putting himself into touch with that older wisdom, because thereby he will more purely express in himself the meaning of that life, and in him, and in others of like meditation, Its wisdom will be kept alive in the world, till the new cycle comes and the mystic fires shine out again in the mysterious respirations and aspirations of time. "Read less, think more," he once advised one of that circle that turned to him for leadership. Why? Because modern books are a confusion of that simplicity; too often a denial of it, or an argumentation about it; but the splendour lies in man, even though a base conception of life dwell in his mind, and by meditation he may evoke it. By meditation he may put himself in the midst of wisdom, and knowledge, even the knowledge considered proper to the test-tubes of modern Science, will flow forth naturally, for the life of the Universe is in him, and in himself, if he can but powerfully centre himself within himself, he will lay hold of that life and understand it. Scientists themselves, indeed, prove this. There was no great "discovery" made by test-tubes or the like apparatus. The history of Science proves well enough that every great discovery came in some rare and lucid intuition, when the knowledge hidden in the depths of man's being, and borne unwittingly by him through his days in some tacit function of that being, suddenly — evoked may be, though not necessarily, by the sight of a little part of the universe working in picture in a test-tube — flashes before his thinking brain. For discoveries, indeed, are less discoveries than recoveries.

So he writes of "The Hero in Man". He who sang of Earth —

> The tender kiss hath memory we are kings
> For all our wanderings,

declares, "There is a spirit in us deeper than our intellectual being which I think of as the Hero in man, who feels the nobility of its place in the midst of all this, and who would fain equal the greatness of perception with deeds as great," and adds in a premonition of the work to which he was so soon to be bidden: "The weariness and sense of futility which often falls upon the mystic after much thought is due to this, that he has not recognized that he must be worker as well as seër, that here he has duties demanding a more sustained endurance, just as the inner life is so much vaster and more intense than the life he has left behind." And again: "Here I may say that the love of the Mother, which, acting through the burnished will of the hero, is wrought to highest uses, is in reality everywhere, and pervades with profoundest tenderness the homeliest circumstance of daily life; and there is not lacking, even among the humblest, an understanding of the spiritual tragedy which follows upon every effort of the divine nature bowing itself down in pity to our shadowy sphere; an understanding in which the nature of the love is gauged through the extent of the sacrifice and the pain which is overcome." In the pale light which plays around such dream-stories as "The Mask of Apollo", and "A Dream of Angus Oge," and "The Story of a Star", there shine the intimations of those things that came to him in early days. In the last, for instance, to the question, "To what end is this life poured forth and withdrawn?" the answer comes: "The end is creation, and creation is joy. The One awakens out of quiescence as we come forth, and knows itself in us; as we return, we cater it in gladness, knowing ourselves." From this, with the faint rhythms of the prose in which these dreams were imaged, he came to the greater dignity of the prose of "The Hero in Man," commensurate as it is with the greater dignity of the thought that man does not need to learn of the hero "by observance of the superficial life and actions of a spiritual teacher," but that "it is only in the deeper life of meditation and imagination that it can be truly realized". So the old writing said that God made man in His own image; and though that image be deflowered and defaced, it may yet be recovered, for the most sordid have the memory of its presence in them. And this it was that William James meant when he said that he knew that F. W. H. Myers was right in what he sought, for it made him more beautiful to look on every day he lived. With such things the builder of the temple came to those who had gathered in its garden. It was an Irish garden. It was not for nothing that the speaker of such words came of the Irish race. We say, when we see men taking the common likeness of a country, that Earth, in different places, subdues men to the local parts of herself, obscuring a brighter mystery with that easy phrase; and, whatever may be the truth of race, we know that there is this strange thing, a thing that defies, and finally disrupts, all imperial ambitions. It was on the hills of Ireland that illumination descended on Æ — on one of that company of hills that guard its shores, and which the race once saw peopled with the Danaan gods, the tribes of the god Dana, the Mother's bright emanations, her mysterious and majestic presences. Therefore when he thinks of the glory that was on the earth, which we know by the wise and great dungs that were sung in it, his mind reverts to the fires that once lit the hills of Erin; and the names of the old heroes come to his lips and what they meant to the race and to the poets of the race arises in his mind. Synge, turning from these things, to which he nevertheless had to revert, might say, "after looking at one of Æ's pictures":

Adieu, sweet Angus, Maeve and Fand,
Ye plumed yet skinny Shee,
That poets played with hand in hand
To learn, their ecstasy.

We'll stretch, in Red Dan Sally's ditch,
And drink in Tubber fair,
Or poach with Red Dan Philly's bitch
The badger and the hare.

Yet it was no poet's fancy they aroused in Æ; but something far nearer to Earth than poaching hares, good and zestful though that might be. "Leaving aside that mystic sense of union with another world and looking only at the tales of battle, when we read of heroes whose knightly vows forbade the use of stratagem in war, and all but the equal strife with equals in opportunity; when we hear of the reverence for truth among the Fianna, 'We the Fianna of Erin never lied, falsehood was never attributed to us' — a reverence for truth carried so far that they did not believe their foemen even could speak falsely — I say that in these days when our public life is filled with slander and unworthy imputation, we might do worse than turn back to that ideal Paganism of the past, and learn some lessons of noble trust, and this truth that greatness of soul alone insures victory to us who live and move and have our being in the life of God."

So when he turns forward to the next inspiration of Earth he writes of "The Awakening of the Fires," from which this quotation is given. For Ireland is not as other countries in Europe. Even as every great Empire of the world has failed at her shores, so every modern movement has left her cold. "The literature of Europe has had but little influence on the Celt in this isle," he says. "Its philosophies and revolutionary ideas have stayed their waves at his coast; they had no message of interpretation for him, no potent electric thought to light up the mystery of his nature." Again in "Nationality and Cosmopolitanism in Art" he says: "The psychic maladies which attack all races when their civilization grows old must needs be understood to be dealt with: and they cannot be understood without being revealed in literature or art. But in Ireland we are not yet sick with this sickness." Turning to our nearest neighbour he says, in "The Awakening of the Fires": "Consider what a thousand years of empire brought to England. Wealth without parallel, but at what expense! The lover of his kind must feel as if a knife were entering his heart when he looks at those black centres of boasted prosperity, at factory, smoke and mire, the arid life and spiritual death. Do you call these miserable myriads a humanity? We look at those people in despair and pity. Where is the ancient image of divinity in man's face: where in man's heart the promptings of the divine? There is nothing but a ceaseless energy without; a night terrible as hell within."

We have our faults in our land; most of us are not blind to them; but the fact that these things are true are their own hope for the future. When the next cycle of inspiration comes, as the cycle of respiration now completes itself, we are readier than any nation. Before the city began to be built — as Æ was soon to set out to that work, and to the preparation for that work — no colossal and revolutionary destruction is necessary, as after a great war colossal and revolutionary destruction will come in every other land. "During all these centuries the Celt has kept in his heart some affinity with the mighty beings ruling in the unseen, once so evident to the heroic races who preceded him. His legends and fairy tales have connected his soul with the inner lives of air and water and earth, and they in turn have kept his heart sweet with hidden influence." And "so this Isle, once called the Sacred Isle and also the Isle of Destiny, may find a destiny worthy of fulfilment: not to be a petty peasant republic, nor a miniature duplicate in life and aims of great material empires, but that its children out of their faith, which has never failed, may realize this immemorial truth of man's inmost divinity, and in expressing it may ray their light over every land."

Lest any should level the old foolish taunt against the dreamer, he is quick to show that he knows the other side of his country also. He can pair discovery with experience. At that time Parnell, the people's "natural choice of hero," had been brought low by an appeal that no Irishman now contemplates without a sense of shame; and he faces this. "I say that where this takes place to any great extent, as it has with us, it is not a land a freeman can think of with pride. It is not a place where the lover of freedom can rest, but he must spend sleepless nights, must brood, must scheme, must wait to strike a blow." It is well not to see only an obverse; but it is well, too, not to see only a reverse; and it is true that when Æ made his discoveries of Man's cosmic life he also, and therewith, made discoveries as an Irishman, for the fairest tree that reaches its leaves to heaven must plant its roots in some portion of the Earth, and the higher it aspires the more deeply must it strike its root.

It needed work ahead. Not to be wise after the event, the signs pointed to the builder of the temple going forth to the city. Writing of W.B. Yeats in "The Poet of Shadows," he said: "We, all of us, poets, artists, and musicians, who work in shadows, must sometime begin to work in substance, and why should we grieve if one labour ends and another begins? I am interested more in life than in the shadows of life, and as Ildathach grows fainter I await eagerly the revelation of the real nature of one who has built so many mansions in the heavens." That was some years before his summons to the city-builders: another of those curious intimations one meets among his discoveries: for the other labour of which he here spoke in ignorance of its existence was soon to begin.

AE Russell: A Study of a Man and a Nation

CHAPTER III

PREPARATIONS

In 1830, at the height of the Land Agitation, a landlord by the name of John Scott Vandeleur, puzzled by the problem of his estates in the County Clare — a problem that was, for him, as rarely for his class, a matter of humanity as well as a matter of rental — and having fallen under the teaching of Robert Owen, decided to take an appropriate and decidedly novel advantage of the execution of his steward by establishing a co-operative society, based on the equally novel principle that a man is not naturally a knave and only accidentally a fool, but primarily a good fellow with an odd chance of splendour and with an enormous faculty of reacting against his circumstances with a fit and meet reply. Since, therefore, anger met anger, denial met denial, and since outrage against human property answered the far deeper outrage against human and national dignity, he decided to organize "The Ralahine Agricultural and

Manufacturing Co-operative Association." It was conducted by him and the upright English secretary he employed with a queer mixture of kindliness, shrewd common sense, and national blatancy. He made over certain portions of land to a community, to be elected in the first instance by the ballot of the tenants, and later to be increased by the ballot of itself, for which, and the houses he had erected, they were to pay by a fixed rental to be paid in kind. He provided stock and implements of husbandry for the community, which belonged to him until such time as the community had sufficient to pay for them, whereupon they became the joint property of the society. No drink, no tobacco, and no gaming were permitted; and a committee of management was elected to control life and work, each night putting up a notice of what each man and woman's work was to be for the following day. Moreover, every manner of labour had its fixed wage, and the community bought of its own store, all profits realizable from the joint husbandry or the joint store to go, firstly, to purchasing the stock and implements provided by the landlord, and then in division among the members.

Together with such and otherwise provisions[3], were certain tendencies not so wise, nor, we may say, at all so disinterested. For the children were to be taught to speak English instead of Irish, in spite of the prohibition of their parents; English country dances were vainly encouraged to displace Irish jigs; and for Harvest-home certain verses were penned, of which the following are the first two:

> The social brotherhood of man
> Alone can bless the boon of birth;

Preparations

And Nature, in her generous plan,
Has taught us how to use the earth.
Chorus
Hail! brothers, hail! in bark, or hut, or hall:
Hail! for each must live for all!

Why should not generous sympathy
Prevail throughout the breathing world,
And o'er the human family
The flag of *Union* float unfurled?

This they were required to sing to the tune of "Rule
Britannia." Nature's generous plan, "Rule Britannia," the
flag of Union and County Clare peasantry in the days
of Land Agitation at Harvest-home, suggest a picture that
would be infinitely humorous were it not so tragic. There
is a certain kind of paternal and national benevolence
that is more profoundly irritating than the most virulent
enmity. However, the County Clare peasantry took very
kindly to the "system" after a very natural suspicion. The
historian of these things says that though, before this time,
they "might be accounted as so many Ishmaelites," bandits,
robbers, murderers, and what-not, they now became keen
and willing, with a fine sense of responsibility and dignity, indefatigable in industry, and requiring no overseer
to see that they worked capably and hard at whatever task
to which they might be appointed by their committee.
Moreover, they displayed a fine communal sense without
any reference to profits, providing for sick and aged, and
going forth in a body to reap the harvests of those who,

through age, were incapable of labour, though such did not belong to their community. Such things were put down to the magic of the "system": they can be explained by a much simpler and more natural magic, that received, as will be seen, an excellent exposition in the old Irish way of life that was deliberately destroyed.

The first question that the mind naturally asks with regard to such a community is touching the end of it all. What would happen if John Scott Vandeleur died or changed his mind? Unhappily John Scott Vandeleur did not heed his own good instruction in the matter of gaming, and in 1833 he fled the country; and the next comer resumed the land, and with it resumed the improvements made upon it by this little deluded Tolstoian community. Another landlord bequeathed certain lands and moneys for the establishment of another such community; but the law set his will aside on the ground of insanity. And so co-operation, even of this mild paternal sort, languished in Ireland for some decades.

Though the experiment proceeded from a paternal benevolence whose habit of mind it is to pay less heed to the desires and motives of humankind than to the formal excellence of its doctrines, it yet hit upon the strong instinct of our race that once erected as wise a conception of civil polity as the world has yet seen. And when in 1889 Horace Plunkett came forward with a solution for Irish agriculture, he hit upon the same instinct, though he came with a proposal that addressed itself directly to the solution of an acute problem and was little concerned with abstract benevolence. There is no hint that at the time he saw what was

implied in his proposals, or what might thereafter be the
flower from the root he had in mind to plant. Ireland was of
old an agricultural people: in 1889 she was so still; not only
because she still clave to Earth with the same ancient affec-
tion, though that was, and is, true, but also because each of
her industries in turn had been deliberately and of foresight
strangled in the interests of English industries. Ireland was of
old, for the main part, a nation of smallholders: in 1889 she
was so still; not now by ancestral continuity but rather by a
particularly malign desire for discontinuity exerted on the
country through centuries of oppression. But where other
people inclined to agriculture could turn it to advantage
by effective organization and better economy in procedure,
Ireland could do little because her farmers had no organization, and were thus, apart from the natural disabilities of
this, the prey of middlemen who sold dearly to them the
raw stuff of their work and bought cheaply from them the
tilth of their labour. There was no remedy. Smallholders
cannot buy the expensive implements with which sowing
and harvest are made speedy and cheap; and therefore they
cannot win the best from the soil, though they would have
to accept the prices decreed by these speedier and cheaper
methods in other parts of the world. Lacking organization,
moreover, they could not even know what these prices
were; or, knowing them, they could not demand them. Yet
whatever they purchased, they had to purchase at a range
of prices decided by a play and interplay in the exchange
of various commodities in a social economy of which they
knew nothing. They were even fortunate when they could
claim that range of prices in their purchase. For the longer

they struggled the poorer they became; the poorer they became the more they fell into the debt of the middleman; and when they fell into his debt he could demand that they should purchase only from him and sell only to him at what prices he in his judgment should decree. The middleman in Ireland thus became a *gaimbin*[4] and the farmer his helot.

The solution to this, as suggested by Horace Plunkett, was simple enough. The human mind always believes that the obvious barely needs statement, whereas the obvious, in a world of tangled interests, demands the hardest battles where the most elaborate perversion, however implausible, will find a host of interested folk to guide it to success or maintain it in power. So Horace Plunkett found it when he suggested that Irish farmers should, instead of acting as hitherto in detached and helpless units, band themselves together in companies, and buy collectively for their collective use, the implements they could not afford to buy separately for their separate use, buy moreover, as corporate bodies could afford to do, directly from the main sources without the interposition of the middleman and sell directly in the world's markets without the interposition of the middleman. Or, as Æ was to put it afterwards, they should recognize that farmers were manufacturers, and as manufacturers they should buy wholesale and sell retail, instead of buying retail and selling wholesale as hitherto; into which advantageous position, however, they could only advance by abandoning their helpless position as detached and separate units and acting co-operatively together.

Simple enough and obvious enough; yet it took long labour before it could win practical acceptance. Men who are in debt are not only men in bondage but also men in fear; and men in fear are they who have lost the certitude or hope of success. That is to say, not only was it necessary that they should be able to clear their books with the local *gaimbin* before they could shake their wills free of his, but they had lost the mental resiliency for initiative. Men who are the heirs of centuries of such abominable oppression as has never yet in history been inflicted by one nation upon another, and the victims of a system that made all attempts to rise seem folly to conceive, will not suddenly arise to strength though an angel be sent to them. Moreover, the *gaimbin* were soon alert. The strings that pull the actions of this world are shaped of gold, and none other are of avail. The *gaimbin* shaped these strings, and a political party needs financing. One of the leaders of that political party, besides, was one of the greatest *gaimbin* in the country; and it was easy to advance the plausible argument that a doctrine of self-help weakens the case for national self-governance, though this plea was eventually surrendered for naked opposition in the interests of the *gaimbin*.

These things shaped themselves from the beginning. Yet, though progress was slow, progress was made. In 1894, the Irish Agricultural Organization Society was formed for the completer organization of the various co-operative societies and agricultural banks that had been established, and for the more vigorous prosecution of the idea. Further organizers and propagandists were required; and in 1897, when Horace Plunkett was looking about for another such organizer, W.B. Yeats suggested to him one who, though he was a mystic and an idealist, besides having published a couple of volumes of poetry, might notwithstanding be supposed to have a little practical experience by the quaint chance of his being an accountant at the drapery house of Pim's. Moreover, a man who could expound the Upanishads, conceivably could expound co-operation. The records of that particular conversation have unfortunately not been preserved. The mind dwells upon the scene with a certain intense satisfaction. The picture of the poet of "The Wind Among the Heeds," speaking with the Vice-President of the Department of Agriculture and Technical Education — for he was soon to arrive at official dignity after a career of tilting at windmills — and recommending as an organizer of co-operation a certain friend of his who was something of a mystic, something of a visionary, something of a poet and prose-writer, but fundamentally, an accountant at a drapery house, has a quiet and peaceful humour; and those who know the persons engaged in that conversation, and the subject thereof, will find that humour deepened by filling in the personal details of that scene. Assuredly, Ireland is the country of all countries in which to live and to work.

The three men concerned, however, were men of intellect, and as in Ireland intellect is not departmentalized the result passes into history. Æ left his desk at Pim's, utterly weary of its soulless monotony, took a bicycle, and set out through Ireland with his evangel. Founding Raffeisen banks in aid of the half-converted or those thereby likely to be converted, addressing the wary, contending with the caviller, refuting the cynic, fighting the usurer, giving a decent man's aid in the matter of pigs, dipping a mystic's pen in ink, indeed, for the betterment of pigs, gathering together co-operative societies in poultry, co-operative creameries, co-operative societies for the purchase of expensive machinery in farm-use, artificial manures scientifically adjusted for differing soils, fodder where necessary, and unadulterated seeds (a subsequent enquiry proved that the seeds then sold to Irish farmers were adulterated up to and over sixty per cent), and pedalling from county to county, through barony after barony, was to be sure new occupation for the mystic, though by no means an untheosophical occupation. That Life is comprised in no thinker's terms needs no saying. That Life to be comprised in a poet's vision requires to be experienced needs insistence, though it seem truism enough, for a good deal of the world's song has been a leisured hobby. And henceforward over Æ's work the smell of turf-reek was to pass, and he who had seen Ireland afar in vision was to look on her with closer and clearer eyes.

The lack of beauty, in its more obvious sense, in his future writing might seem to suggest a lack of continuity in his life. Other superficial signs there are that seem to suggest that same lack of continuity; for that rare prose, so delicate in its rhythms and rising at its height to an impassioned ecstasy, began to be less frequently heard; song was heard less often on his lips, and when it revisited him its themes were more obvious, less incommensurable, and, indeed, it was oftener a noble speechcraft than the craft of singing; the visions and mystical experiences of the "household," in the course of time, died away, though they recurred at whiles with a new power, and with their passing the painter, in course of time, turned from their record to the more familiar sights of the earth. A workaday directness took their place; and the mind that was acute in translating the obscure experiences of the spirit in terms of the intellect without essential loss of meaning, turned at last to public debate with a shrewd humour and ability that foemen learned to respect and which he himself lusted to display. In a superficial sense it might be said that a change had occurred. Changes always occur, and are always superficial, when a man turns another side of his being toward life.

Looked at more closely, it is the continuity rather than the discontinuity that reveals itself; and to miss this is not only to miss the meaning of Æ's days, but the very curious thing that happened to the I.A.O.S. Horace Plunkett, who had been a rancher in America and who came of a family habituated to public affairs, mixed the two things by coming forward with a very simple, and therefore startling, solution of the difficulties of the Irish farmer. It was of those difficulties he had thought, and it was the problem those difficulties presented he wished to unriddle. He did unriddle them, very satisfactorily: so satisfactorily that out of the difficulties of the Irish farmer sprang an idea that became an inspiration to farming as far removed as the Western States of America and India. It was sound economics applied to a disastrously uneconomical situation; and it was meant as no more. The very fact that it meant the breaking up of usury — and a particularly virulent form of usury — proves how sound the economics were, for the usurer is an economic pest. But, in the course of organizing his economic scheme, while under the incantations of a poet he was induced to commit a part of his scheme to quite another sort of a man with quite another outlook on life.

This does not mean that Æ organized better or worse than any of the other organizers, or that his organizing differed in any essential from the instructions according to which he proceeded. Even had it done so — as might have been the case for all the world will ever know — he and his bicycle had to pass on their baronial way, and head-quarters might be trusted to produce uniformity. But who was this traveller through the baronies, and what was the impact of his present experiences on his past discoveries? Though we cannot answer for Sir Horace Plunkett's soul, we may assume that whenever he unriddled his problem, in his own day of organizing and propaganda, unriddled it was, and the farmers' situation so far became a straighter, a neater, a more prosperous, and also a manlier, affair. This other man, however, had lived quite another sort of life; he had made spirirtual discoveries, and had caught or had cast them in beauty, to make them his own and to pass them to others. Was an uneconomic problem unriddled with a suitable economic reply the be-all and end-all of his organizing? He had in vision seen life as a steady flame mounting up fragrantly to the throne of God, where the light was like a cloud, dense and unbearable; he had heard His Voice borne through the universe and in chord on chord of music build up the souls of Earth and her children, with the fine memory in them of the Beauty from whence they came and wherein only they could live if Life was to be more than breathing; he had seen Life softly eradicate and disperse the troubled clouds of perplexity with the vision of auspicious destinies yet to serve, and with a troubled and travelling past growing into the triumph of a life yet to be; he had seen Power silently shining forth, Love transfiguring, Beauty transforming, Being mantled in an ecstasy of flame; he had seen the thought of God in man's body and the passions of God for beauty and holiness beating swiftly in his blood; he had seen these things, not as a dreamer's dream, but as the very certitudes of his soul; and he had seen Ireland where the hills had once shone with mystic fires, a precious place, where in the next mysterious rhythm of earth glory was to come again, and a new teaching go forth, as once of old, through the world: was he answered with the answering of a farmer's problem, of pure seeds, of wholesale buying and retail selling, and a victory over the stultifying, blighting usurer squatting astraddle across from the nation's life?

What was it he saw as he and his bicycle went on their travels? How did it compare with what he had seen in the vision? When he matched vision with sight what was the reaction of his mind after the co-operative organizer had completed his task and replaced disorder with order and disunion with union? The thought of men returning to wisdom and dignity as they returned to the bosom of Mother, had shone as a fair thing before his eye; but now as he went through the country, though he found wisdom and dignity there in the heart of the same, and even more acute, poverty that in the cities implied squalor and vulgarity, yet he saw young men and young women streaming away to cities — cities not in Ireland, but in America, each district in Ireland having its counterpart in some city in America:

Aran passing to Chicago, Achill to Cleveland, and so forth. Life had fallen from its ancient usage; the stir of the modern world had brought unrest; the praise of education had come, with withered scraps of knowledge that were extolled as a kind of currency, to be changed later in life for hard cash, so noble was the conception of it, though after-days sadly belied those pretensions; the rail and the telegraph had narrowed the world; so that with lowered values of Life and a heightened interest and curiosity a life near to Earth connoted nothing but intolerable tedium. The herded cities shone like glittering palaces. Values were lost: dignity and wisdom, though they still splendidly remained, were lightly esteemed for the most part beside the modern counterparts of success and passing information. A naturally aristocratic people do not easily change; but the change was astir; and the cities promised information — true or false, what did it matter, so long as it helped life to slip away unnoticed and helped gregariousness? — and the cities tempted with success, though it was true that rumour had it that this success came hardly and only to a few.

Added to that was the hardihood of it all. A life near to Earth connoted not only tedium but a desperate struggle, a nightmare of drudgery, of failure and debt, of malnutrition and depressed vitality, and thus of disease and early decrepitude. For not only had values changed, standards also had changed. Speedier methods, a completer organization, a better use of the scientific discoveries more easily available in places where farming was conducted by syndicates, were demanded of a life near to Earth before its continuance was even possible. Economics have fallen into disrepute among healthy men because of the type of person who conducts their discussion. It was once, for instance, gravely propounded in a certain School of Economics as to "whether a margin of unemployment was not necessary in order that in times of trade prosperity a larger body of labour might not in that emergency be called upon"; to which the only honourable answer was, not to hear and discuss the thesis, but to strike the lecturer upon the mouth, and, after having picked him up, to point out to him that by "a larger body of labour" he really meant starving men. Economics, however, means mutual aid; and mutual aid means decent comradeliness; and decent comradeliness means fair living; and those who discuss economics in terms of cash instead of in terms of men are those who do, or those who hope to, or those who are hired by those who do or hope to, trample on their fellows. Pedantry is a confusion of clear thinking; but sometimes that lack of clear thinking arises from something not at all so innocent as frailty or clumsiness of mind.

The cynic, conscious or unconscious, sneers at the poet's terms; but the poet's terms always justify themselves by the disaster that ensues when they are neglected. The poet had spoken of a life near to Earth; he had seen Man in a high comradeship of Life. What now did he find? He saw that the life near to Earth became impossible because that high comradeship had been replaced by exploitation; and then the poet became economist. He saw goods becoming coin of the realm, with a most subtle confusion resulting; he saw an ancient form of barter conducted as an elaborate trick instead of as a simple interchange. He saw the farmer egg buying the *gaimbin* tea, the egg at well below current wholesale rates (was there not a debt outstanding?) and the tea at retail rate, bearing twenty to twenty-five per cent profit. He might also have seen the smallholder farmer smoking his *duidin* till the bowl blistered his lips with the heat, and taking an egg (value two or three halfpennies) to buy a pipe (value one halfpenny), and without any remedy. He saw, as he says, "hordes of keen-witted business men" who "began to handle" the farmer's "produce; they occupied all the roads to the markets, they did all his business for him, fixed the prices for his stock and crops, and saw to it that riches should not prove hereafter a stumbling-block at his entrance to Heaven. Those who brought his requirements into the district had the same watchful care over his chances of future happiness. He was doubly saved. I do not say," he adds, "that these forces acted with conscious enmity to the farmer. They were mostly efforts to help him, as well intentioned as the elephant who, seeing some motherless chickens, said, 'I will be a mother to the poor little things,' and lay down on them to keep them warm. Tragic-comic legend thought it unnecessary to develop the further history of that clutch. The Irish elephants have lain down heavily on the farmers, and have obliterated many of the brood they have intended to bear[5] — obliterating also the life near Earth, the dignity of man, the hero in man, the renewal of youth, the intimations of splendour and the high comradeship and divine purpose, in all at least that was outwardly visible.

The poet had sung of Earth that her "tender kiss hath memory we are kings for all our wanderings"; but the busi-

ness done on Earth's bosom had such consequences that
the only chance her child had of realizing himself as a king
was by a good dose of porter or whisky. It is easy to blame
that child; it is right to blame him; and Æ has some exqui-
site scorn for the seekers after as well as for the ennobled
purveyors of that immagical summoner of hidden kingship;
but the follies of man are often an inverted wisdom, and
are at most an escape from a life that he is only wishful to
deny as his. No man felt a king when drunk who had not
a reasonable chance of realizing that kingship when sober
if only things were reasonably ordered. Drunkenness, when
not a physical disease or an unhappy (or happy) accident,
is generally the result of misery or malnutrition; and the
dweller on the bosom of Earth coming to a sordid town
on a fair-day, with a life behind him and before him of
hardship and monotony and unremitting struggle, with
only potatoes and bread to eat, and tea to drink so strong
that it quelled hunger by reaction, fleeced by the higgler at
home in his petty sales and swindled at the fair in his larger
purchases by dealers and jobbers with a prearranged scale
of prices that he knew to be below the rates prevailing, but
reduced to helplessness by their parasites the tanglers and
blockers, in debt to the *gaimbin* and with rent or instalment
falling due — such a man turning to whisky is not at all a
confutation of his kingship, or of the warrior-hero or bard
in him, as he will occasionally display in fine order, with
seanchas or cudgel.

So the poet conceiving of civilization, ancient or modern,
and especially of days before the bragged-of "dawn of civilization," was faced by an order with nothing whatsoever that

was civil in it, except perhaps the feelings of the drunken king faced by the hills and the sky or the rolling stretch of bog on the following morning. What was the impact on him of this new discovery? How did he face his discoveries of the past, of the "household" and the mystical society, with the footing beneath him of his discoveries as an organizer of co-operation?

After some years of organizing, he was appointed assist-ant-secretary to the I.A.O.S. Then in 1905 he was appointed the editor of the official organ of the I.A.O.S., *The Irish Homestead*. For a while he continued the tradition of that organ by dealing with matters essential to homestead and farmer. But even as the "feel" of a shillelagh in the hand of some men is fatal to order, so the "feel" of a pen in the hand of a poet is fatal to disorder. The poet arose again now, in his new guise as economist. Matching discovery with discovery he faced his past with his present, and undertook to devise a state of affairs, by the shrewd application of common sense, in which his old dreams could become possible by the adoption, and expansion, of the very economic gospel he had been sent to preach.

In view of the result, it is right to remember how this came to be. When it is said that he "undertook to devise a state of affairs," that does not mean that Athena sprang full-armed from the head of this particular Zeus. The obstetrics erred, as a point of fact, on the other side of inhumanity. It was difficult to say what portion of the anatomy of the new social order was going to be presented next. Our Zeus himself was in ignorance. It was much later that he became his own midwife, and patted Athena into shapeliness and order. The seed of the new experience on the ovum of the old vision put him in labour for many years, even while he dealt with what are called the exigencies of modern journalism. There was no premeditation as to the result, except in so far as the mind works by a tacit and orderly wisdom beyond cognizance of its own brain. The procedure was simply the answering of questions that arose in his mind, induced in main part by the weekly problems that affected the Irish farmer. It is important to note that fact, inasmuch as the social order he evolved was the counterpart in modern times of something that had existed before in the history of the race, before the stranger had kicked his way brutishly through the land. Our Zeus himself did not know this, till some few of his friends saw the likeness and pointed out to his delighted paternal gaze that Athena was a re-birth not a birth, a re-birth of race wisdom. And then the mind suddenly remembers that about a year before he had joined the I.A.O.S., thinking of the past glory of Ireland and of "The Awaking of the Fires," he had written this sentence: "In hoping for another such day I do not of course mean the renewal of the ancient order, but rather look for the return of the same light which was manifest in the past." It is not every man, to be sure, who is permitted to be both Zeus and Prometheus.

Therefore it is difficult to see of what sort Athena is in the strange labours of her birth in the columns of *The Irish Homestead* week by week; it is comelier to avert our eyes till she be patted and cleaned and reduced to some kind of tentative order in the pages of "Co-operation and Nationality," published seven years later. It is a remarkable book: probably the first piece of thinking from facts rather than from the terminology of other books, in economic literature. It was born of work; not of reading in a study. In it, he faces his old visions bravely, and finds them the truer because of what his further experience has shown him. "Nature," he says, "has no intention of allowing her divine brood, made in the image of Deity, to dwindle away into a crew of little, feeble, feverish city folk. She has other and more grandiose futures before humanity if ancient prophecy and our deepest, most spiritual, intuitions have any truth in them." That becomes the base of his thinking. Sir Horace Plunkett had already decreed as the triple watchword of the co-operative movement, "Better farming, better business, better living." It was a statesmanlike watchword. But Æ, seeing further, sees more deeply, and eliminates any possible littleness of conception, eliminating therewith the things that inevitably lead to degradation of personal and national life.

The life near Earth is deeper and more spiritual. How is it to be ordered so that this may approve itself in fact? If the spiritual life of man be deeper and truer than a material compromise with sloth and selfishness, and spiritual and physical degradation — that is to say, if it be better, not as a pleasing transcendentalism the surrender of which only creates a sentimental pang, but as a cardinal thing which, if it cannot approve itself in experience, must be bravely cast aside as a delusion, and every preacher thereof in pulpits stoned as liar and trickster — what is to be done with a state of affairs which, by its very continuance, denied that fact? That was the challenge to the poet. Was he, like the most of poets and preachers and professors of faiths, to bow his mind to truth and square his life with its denial; or was he to take up the challenge he himself had offered to himself?

Already as organizer for the I.A.O.S., he had answered a part of his problem. The Life near Earth had become impossible. Why? Because men lived lives of individual selfishness, suspicion and greed, each man separate from his fellows and struggling against his fellows: a state of affairs the baseness of which was disguised by those who chanced to be successful in the sordid game by the fair phrase "competitive interests" that was cast as a cloak about it; but a state of affairs that worked itself out in desperation for the huge mass of those struggling and separated men. Directly they were called to the nobler conception of mutual aid, what happened? Not only did they at once stand on a nobler plane of life; not only did the greater part of them for the first time in their lives realize in little measure the teaching of the Christ; but at once their economic disabilities disappeared. The higgler, the dealer, the jobber, the tangler, the blocker, the middleman, and the *gaimbin*, were at once cut away; and the click was heard in every place of a machinery that began to fall together as a harmonious unit because the key for its well-working had been discovered. The co-operative societies, each member of which in working for and with, instead of against, his fellows, worked the better and the more freely for himself, began to federate together for greater power and freedom. Especially was this necessary when the army of middlemen, finding they could no longer put their hands into their fellows' pockets, threw the whole weight of their earlier winnings against them in naked fight and bought

misrepresentation. Then the co-operative federations created the Irish Agricultural Wholesale Society, guaranteeing
to themselves thus the bottom prices in the purchase of
machinery and goods and guaranteed purity of seeds. And
from top to bottom, men became their own economic
masters when they ceased to desire economic mastery over
others or refused to permit others to assume economic
mastery over themselves, and decided in free debate and
election the vital concerns of their lives instead of having
these decided by others.

It was better business; and therefore made a life on the
land more possible. It was saner and manlier; and so it
helped the dignity of man; for even as the little Ralahine
Society turned out to gather the harvest of the infirm so
these co-operative societies began to realize civic duties and
responsibilities. Men of sharply divided political opinions,
at the very height of political controversies, acted together,
not only in business interests, but with a civic purpose; and
instead of dividing all their profits began to allocate some
portion of these to public purposes within the community,
beginning therewith intelligently to discuss those public
purposes. In other words, the co-operative societies became
rural communities. Out of the disorder that had prevailed, a
civilization emerged. The men who had struggled pitifully
against conditions too hard for them, preserving, however,
for the most part (as it is part of the instinct of our race to
preserve) a dignity and fellow-kindliness amazing under the
circumstances, now became citizens. They were compelled
to think for themselves; and that gave them new interests.
Prosperity quickened those interests. A larger reach of sci-

ence came in with the chemistry of manures and the soil. A better knowledge of peoples and events at a distance came with the ability to reach that distance directly in selling power. Nationality meaning now a tissue of live interests instead of a medley of ancient catchwords, clearer political thinking resulted. Better independence and a stronger dignity resulted from the right to take the responsibility of important decisions; which concluded in logic what began in justice with the land agitation, for the imposition of the middleman, and especially the *gaimbin* variety, was now broken as the imposition of the landlord had been broken. As men became their own masters, the pride of life arose. And the basis of all this was a rural community where, if a man were prosperous, it was not as a result of exploiting his fellows, but by helping them in the degree in which he helped himself.

So the conception slowly and tentatively emerged that gave the economist's answer to the poet — emerged hand in hand, and pace by pace, with their results in fact. "Sometimes," he says, "one feels as if there were some higher mind in humanity which could not act through individuals, but only through brotherhoods and groups of men"; and here were brotherhoods and groups working out some part of that higher mind. Yet, so far, they were farming, and not social, brotherhoods, civic only in some chance extension of their powers. Until the farming brotherhood was made also a social brotherhood, the further possibility was little more than hinted. "Fine character in a race is evolved and not taught. It is not due to copybook headings or moral maxims given to the youth of the country. It arises from the structure of society and the appeal it makes to them." So he writes, so simply and truly; and our bitter history is such that "we have not had a social order since the time of the clans," for the stranger's ruthless foot of set design kicked that social order to pieces, though it left fragments of it dispersed about the country. He says, "We will yet see the electric light and the telephone in rural districts, and the village hall with a hum of friendship in it," but the village hall had first to be made, and a company to avail itself of that hall in other than as a promiscuous charity, half welcomed, half resented, had first to be ordered. The demand for it exists, caused by the modern tedium with an insufficient mental life — or as Sir Horace Plunkett has said[6]: "If the domestic and social life of the country does not advance with its economic life, all but the dullards will fly to the town." But first a society must be created, and behind that again a social order, and behind that a sufficient social conception. For it was not at random that Æ wrote: "I hate to hear of stagnant societies who think because they have made butter well that they have crowned their parochial generation with a halo of glory, and can rest content with the fame of it all, listening to the whirr of steam separators and pouching in peace of mind the extra penny a gallon for their milk. And I dislike the little groups who meet a couple of times a year and call themselves co-operators, because they have got their fertilizers more cheaply, and have done nothing else."

So "The United Irishwomen"[7] arose, for "we cannot build a rural civilization in Ireland without the aid of women." It began with, or rather was awoken and crystallized by Æ as he, week by week in *The Irish Homestead*, faced the problems that he the poet put to himself the economist and practical farmer. It worked from the house toward the village hall. It sought to free women from onerous work on the land, and succeeded in some places with the co-operation of the men; it organized nursing in home and village; it taught domestic economy and hygiene; it gave care to the woman's part of agricultural life, such as poultry, home-dairying, pig-breeding, bee-keeping, and cottage-gardening; and it created a social life. Such things it did: and does, for the movement has a long furrow to plough. It is a work most full of pitfalls; for in such work it is easy to de-nationalize; and to de-nationalize is to other-nationalize, and finally alienize, in both meanings of the word. Yet as the work approaches the village hall it joins, in feet as well as in theory, with the Gaelic League; with which it must finally co-operate — as indeed the whole of the co-operative movement must finally work with the Gaelic League in rebuilding a distinctively Irish State, drawing on its own separate sources and traditions, despite the Statutes of Kilkenny.

Thus, the economist tentatively felt his way, relying, on no path blazed in text-books, but on his own inner light, hardly knowing where he would finally emerge. Yet there was one part of the city-building to which he had been called that he had not canvassed in his thinking. That was the slums of citydom. They lay outside his work and his thinking. He was not, however, suffered to forget them. All of Ireland, for good or ill, had to be reckoned with before the thought of the National Being could justly ensue. And so Æ came to one of the most honourable moments of his life.

At the very moment that farm labourers were on strike, under the direction of the Irish Transport Union, against the farmers for whom he had thought and laboured, under the same direction a great and historic strike broke out in Dublin. Rather, it was not a strike but a lock-out in which the employers federated to break the Union, and reminded the workers that while the strife continued the masters could rely on their three square meals a day while the workers could but starve. Never was such unanimity procured in Ireland. Political parties and journals forgot their strife, and rallied against the workers. In a world of debased, because commercialized, honour, money commands; and money commanded. To the honour of Dublin poets be it said that they rallied to the workers; but they were a small and helpless company. Then Æ's "being went up in a blaze." He came into the fray with an open letter "To the Masters of Dublin." At a meeting organized in London to help the workers, apologizing first to his countrymen for departing from his custom by speaking on an English platform while yet the wrongs done to his country were unredressed, he attacked those who deserted the poor when their Master would have been with them. Hatred assailed him on every side, for his entry into the fray had lifted the issue on to the plane of ideals: he had made the issue one of faith espoused or deserted. Speaking in conversation at that time, he spoke of himself as a psychic person who felt hate striking on him like darts from every quarter; and it was idle to remind him that that hatred, where ignorant, was pitiful, for the poor, were they but rightly informed, would aid their fellows in poverty, and that where it was not ignorant it was contemptible, since it sprang from monetary interests; for he knew that already.

The storm rolled by — not in honour. It left, however, two results. His ideas had spread: the thought of a Co-operative Commonwealth defined itself on both sides. Few words were more frequently heard in the ranks of the workers: it took a higher rank in their thoughts than even the question of increased wages with men who were starving. A new thought had come to them: a thought of the State, which if it be not based on fellowship in control, in ideas, and in profits, must be based on exploitation, against which, rather than against this or that scale of wages, they were revolting. The system of "wagery," inherent in them till that time for the lack of any other system that seemed possible, received its first blow; and that idea captured other minds than those of the workers. But a new thought came to Æ. Rather a new challenge came to the poet, to the man before whom Life was something other than an accepted baseness, a commerce in sordure. He accepted the challenge. He began to think out the National Being anew from that point.

CHAPTER IV

A NATION, A STATE; A STATE, A NATION

Of old among the many secret names by which Ireland was known to her children, there was one that arrests the mind with its mysterious faith. That name is *Inis Fáil*: the Isle of Destiny. There have been times, with a bull's hoof planted in her face, when that strange appellation has seemed to be a consummate cynicism: there are pages in her history that it is scarcely possible to read. There are times also, even when she has seemed at the depth of enforced degradation, when that title comes to wear a quite curious significance.

Such a time was the rise and culmination of the nine-teenth century. Every kind of brutality and humiliation was visited upon her, until it seemed that no nation could emerge from the ordeal in which malignity had subdued her. And yet it is true that her very disabilities then saved her from the blight, the deeper, the seeming ineradicable blight, that visited some other nations. Early in that century a poet whom we claim as an Irishman, and an O'Neill moreover, sang —

> I will not cease from mental fight,
> Nor shall my sword sleep in my hand
> Till we have built Jerusalem
> In England's green and pleasant land;

but when we survey England now, and ask how shall a fair State be made of her, the question at once arises, what shall be done with the monstrous cities, built on miles of slumdom, that blister the fair side of Earth, and make so many of her mortal-kind to seem less men than a hopeless putrefaction of humanity? Even as Blake sang one of the fairest shires of the "green and pleasant land" was nearing a time when it would be turned into one vast clinker-patch, and its men, a sturdy race of copyholders farming the fields and cultivating a home industry, turned into wage-slaves, living in darkened streets, their faces stamped with the image of the god they were enforced to serve, passing in their deadened multitudes into the midst of whirring machinery at the blast of a steam-whistle, and passing out again at another blast into homes where no light comes, no flowers shine, and green fields are first an unimagined splendour and finally an undesired freedom. There are no green fields: there are only miles and miles of clinkers.

A Nation, a State: A State, a Nation

There is no sunlight and blue sky: there is only smoke belched out from the steeples of the new temples man has built to his new god. And in the midst of this scene, and under this dark panoply, the tenement-house from which they issue, the foul factories where they labour for some begrudged pittance, and the gin-palace where they forget, comprise the last form of civilization that man, made in the image of God, has devised for the just display of that image. Yet man does display the image of God: whatever god he serves, that image will he display.

To what end, one asks? If some fire of God swept away this ghastly hell it would take three generations of green fields and blue skies to recover what was lost; and to what end shall men be blasted in their souls, and the fair face of Earth be despoiled? That some cotton mills in India, serving their country satisfactorily and well, should be ruined by being undersold in their own markets, and more misery caused out there? A fair goal this, indeed: to debase Life at one end of the world in order to be able to debase it more effectually at the other end! No: but, in plain terms, that some score of men may amass their millions of hard cash, and thereby become as degraded in their own minds as they demand that the minds of their slaves shall be degraded.

Blasphemy? Atheism? It is right maybe to revive these ancient terms; but it is very strange that men in *Inis Fáil* should be called upon to rebuild their State with the hell before them out of which other nations have won their success. Only in two places in Ireland has this terrible conception at all established itself; and in one of them the full horror faced Æ in the midst of one of the bitterest industrial struggles of modern times. There was little of it that he could have evaded, such was the effect on him. The sight of Liberty Hall on a bleak winter's evening, teeming in every part with hungry men and women waiting for soup and bread tickets, men and women, actually in their thousands, clustered on ill-lit and grimy stairs and along murky passages, coming from the very depths of Life, was a sight that can as easily be forgotten as described. Nothing proved more highly the honour of Dublin than their infallible courtesy and kindliness and dignity — dignity, even though the wearer of that dignity were waiting hungrily for a ticket that would entitle him to food. Nothing proved it better, unless it were a cluster of men and women, poets and writers for the most part, who met there, waiting for a task that might be found for them. Among these was Æ; and even had any man the desire to forget these things, having once seen them, it would be hard to purchase the faculty of forgetfulness save with the costly payment of cynicism.

So in the coming months in *The Irish Homestead* he took up the new challenge. In "Co-operation and Nationality," dealing carefully with the beginnings of things, chiefly rural, he had said, "No country can marry any particular solution of its problems and live happily ever afterwards," but now as he struck more deeply towards the roots of national being, and embraced the whole existence of the State, a finer certitude, a more assured conviction, marks his attitude. Yet that attitude is the same. The man is the same. A man's spiritual discoveries are the only certitudes he knows in a world in flux, for they are his insight into the world of which this world of the senses is but a partial appearance. "The spiritual question is the only one," he had said. He says it yet, though his present concern is to devise a State that shall fit the most rigorous requirements, that shall even be, if we so choose to regard it, abreast with modern thinking. It is for the spirit of the nation he is concerned when thinking of the State in which it shall be adequately housed. Civilizations, even when they be least civil (and maybe chiefly then), are the expression in outward fact of the inhabiting soul within. Civilizations also, it is worthy of note, help to mould and fashion that soul by the conceptions on which they are based. To the wise statesman the nationality makes the State, or it becomes an empty doctrinaire shell that is soon neglected; but the wise statesman also remembers that the State makes the nationality. States are not emitted from a fertile brain as constitutions may be, as the Abbé Sieyès so admirably proved by example; for the outward circumstance is created by an indwelling soul and intellectual life. Hence Æ's impatience with what he calls pseudo-military bodies that muster they know not what for: though in this, despite the essential justice of what he says, he over-rashly assumes that the lack of a fine intellectual consciousness supposes the equal lack of a dawning soul, thus brushing aside what should be examined because it gives little of that which he rightly and imperiously demands. It may be true, as he says, that feelings do not presuppose thoughts; but feelings, if they be clean and healthy, may define themselves into thoughts if a thoughtful man identify himself with them, as they assuredly never will if thoughtful men deride them. It is to the high credit of Æ, that he combined clear vision with clear thinking, suffering in himself neither the learned antics of lecture-rooms or round-tables nor the vague inchoate sentiments of the manifold organizations that exist in the country.

It profits a nation nothing if it gain a whole Empire and lose its own soul. It is not to Rome we look for a memorable beauty as we look to Athens; and the Roman wars that lusted for things that were not Roman, and whose crushing impoverished the world by just so much individuality, have not the honour of the Greek wars that defended things that were Grecian. Rome exacted brute dominance; it demanded fealty in the only form in which States value it, in hard cash; but every Roman poet and prose-writer gave intellectual fealty to Greece. Even while Athens was under the heel of the Roman brute-power, Athenic intellect and beauty were masters in Rome. And Æ, enamoured of the things that signify, is not solicitous for the trappings of power on Ireland's behalf but anxious for such an awakening of spiritual life as will build up a notable beauty in the land. Already Ireland had won a fealty from other lands; and that fealty had come of work done partly under his own hand; for the making of a rural civilization, in all the departments of living, had attracted deputations from many places, who had returned home to imitate the things they had seen. To win such a tribute for one's country is a worthy ambition for noble men. A nation that can win such a tribute has dominion, without a single official hired to enforce it; it has governance, without a single soldier to leave its shores; but an Empire of this sort — the only sort that stirs a mind enfranchised from an ancient circus-pomp — can only be gained when a nation has gained its own soul, its nationality, and has housed it in a State fit to receive it.

But what came they out for to see? We know, for they have told us; but we might have guessed had they kept their secret. They came to see a new up-growing civilization that was answering the hardest problem of the modern world, the problem of a life on the land; answering it by making it successful and desirable; and answering it, not by the financial lordship of one man over another, but by the mutual aid of the whole community governing itself, where the prosperity of one man advantaged his fellows, and where the loss of one man weakened the community. Addressing one such delegation Æ said: "We often hear the expression 'the rural community,' but where do we find rural communities? There are rural populations, but that is altogether a different thing. The word 'community' implies an association of people having common interests and common possessions, bound together by laws and regulations which express these common interests and ideals and define the relation of the individual to the community. Our rural populations are no more closely connected, for the most part, than the shifting sands on the seashore. Their life is almost entirely individualistic. There are personal friendships, of course, but few economic or social partnerships. Everybody pursues his own occupation without regard to the occupation of his neighbours. If a man emigrates, it does not affect the occupation of those who farm the land all about him. They go on ploughing and digging, buying and selling, just as before. They suffer no perceptible economic loss by the departure of half a dozen men from the district. A true community would, of course, be affected by the loss of its members. A co-operative society if it loses a dozen members, the milk of their cows, their orders for fertilizers, seeds, and feeding-stuffs, receives serious injury to its prosperity.…That is the difference between a community and an unorganized population."[8]

Yet what of the cities, since cities must be? "If we build our civilization," he says, speaking of cities, "without integrating labour into its economic structure, it will wreck that civilization; and it will do that more swiftly today than a thousand years ago, because there is no longer the disparity of culture between high and low which existed in past centuries." In truth it is doing so now, for that very cause; and it will do so with startling rapidity after a great war. Already the change is in progress. Men are demanding to fix the terms and conditions under which they will labour; they are drawing together in unions that are rapidly becoming guilds to enforce these things, and they bring statesmen to hear and solicit them. Soon, and inevitably, they will demand to elect the captains of their labour; and thus inevitably, sooner or later, into the hands of these guilds will pass the industries with which they are concerned. It needs no amazing prevision to perceive these things. They pursue their way with a certain high honour, to which men prove their folly, and darker things than folly, when they shut their eyes. The hireling knows, for instance — as only they know who have experienced it in a continued bitterness that darkens the sun — the deep dishonour done him by the insecurity of his employment, when, for a little displeasure, he may be sent out to starve, he and those who look to his hand for food; and a thousand are willing to forgo weeks of wages, with the chance of never getting back their posts, for one man who is lightly dismissed. Half the strikes of modern times have been, not for wages, but for principles; and when men by their thousands are willing to lose all for a principle it is time for the poet, not indeed to cavil, but to rub his eyes, and stare, and wonder if his kingdom be coming.

So this poet started up when he heard that most of the working men in Dublin had gone out to starvation rather than be ordered not to join a Union that they, till then, never had had a thought of joining, and to sign a document giving a pledge to that effect. Here already was the makings of a community; and an honourable community. If such could be made part of an economic community in the city, decreeing for itself as the rural community was beginning to do, and in like fashion creating its own prosperity without permitting the exploitation of itself, here then were the two parts of the Co-operative Commonwealth. Common-wealth! Æ has written with the bitterness many have felt of those who speak of the increasing prosperity of a country, judging that prosperity by statistics that signify nothing to the people at large — indeed that signify, in the present framework of society, and inevitably signify, more freedom enslaved and more decency debauched. To speak so is to speak as they did who turned Lancashire in England into a clinker-patch and degraded its manhood, in order that increased statistics should swell the pockets of a few. In Ireland, that example is before us while we seek nobler destinies to serve. Wealth is not national wealth if it pass only to a few and give those few power to exploit their fellows. It is not so in the economic sense. It is not so even in the political sense, for in all countries men become less national in the degree in which they amass riches. Wealth is only estimable when it is a commonwealth; and what is called industrial development, when it does not signify industry developed in a commonwealth, signifies national loss and not gain whatever the trade returns may say.

It is the custom to bend the knee to the faith of the idealist in an elaborate cynic fealty that assumes the sheer impracticability of the schemes he so bravely devises; and it is not the least crafty trick by which the exploiter fobs off enquiry into the first principles of the business of Life. Yet these things have been justified of life. Farmers have co-operated on just such impracticable principles; stripped away middlemen and exploiters; and created, out of desperate poverty, a wealth which is a commonwealth. "I am familiar with a district," says Æ, "It was one of the most wretchedly poor districts in Ireland. The farmers were at the mercy of the gombeen traders and the agricultural middlemen. Then a dozen years ago a co-operative society was formed.... The reign of the gombeen man is over. The farmers control their own buying and selling. Their organization markets for them the eggs and poultry. It procures seeds, fertilizers, and domestic requirements. It turns the members' pigs into bacon. They have a village hall and an allied women's organization. They sell the products of the women's industry. They have a co-operative band, social gatherings, and concerts. They have spread out into half a dozen parishes. They have gone southward to A—— with their propaganda and eastward towards F——, and in half a dozen years in all that district, previously without organization, there will be well-organized farmers' guilds, concentrating in themselves all the trade of their district, having meeting-places where the opinion of the members can be taken; having machinery, committees, and executive officers to carry out whatever may be decided on, and having funds, or profits, the joint property of the community, which can be drawn upon to finance their undertakings." Another such guild of farmers, anticipating an inevitable development, has undertaken the supply of electricity to a neighbouring town from the generating plant for their machinery. Such things have been done, issuing from and emerging into ideals, but wrought in healthy economic success.

The question Æ faces is: How shall this be done in the complexity of modern cities? Here again it is right to be reminded of things that are being done elsewhere. In Italy, workmen's guilds own and conduct industries. They display no parsimony in the payment of competent managers and general directors; but such managers and directors are responsible to a guild of the workers who understand the conditions of their industry, who own the industry in which each of them has his particular function, and not to a company of shareholders ignorant of the conditions, and therefore easily manipulated. This is the counterpart in the factory of what the farmers had wrought in the fields of Ireland. The farmers of Ireland, if not free, have at least in their power now the beginnings of their freedom. But how may workers in factories win an equal freedom?

And here Æ displays a shrewd tactical wisdom. The farmer first captured the organization of his manufactures by the guild he created for that purpose, and then, having the guild, used it for the direct purchase of his requirements on the farm and in the homestead: the middleman who bought from him went first, and the middleman who sold to him followed in due course. Plainly, the worker in the city cannot do this. It would be to court certain failure if a guild of workmen erected a factory co-operatively owned. The requisite experience would not be with them in a complex state of affairs. A huge power of finance would be wielded against them. They would find, not only that they would not sell so cheaply as their opponents, who would be willing at once to pool finances and run at a loss to break them; but they would not be able to sell at all, for the distributive shops would be forced by the big manufacturers, acting together, not to stock co-operative goods under pain of having higher prices levied against them, by a withdrawal of discounts if not by direct increase. The peril of that course must not be considered: not at once. The worker in the city must invert the procedure of the farmer. He must first create his distributive stores; then, having that outlet, create his guild factories; and make his distributive stores discriminate against the goods that do not come from such guild-owned factories, as the manufacturers would have done against him if he had at first challenged competition.

If trade unions, instead of conducting a series of strikes that are often unsuccessful, and which even when successful only erect a temporary new platform of wages that will soon be submerged as competition advances to a new level, were to employ their funds in creating co-operative stores and in compelling their members to deal exclusively at them, they would soon create a new economic dignity for workers. In times of strike, they would consume their own funds, because inasmuch as trade union tickets would only be available at the trade union co-operative stores, the separate funds of the trade unions, instead of being depleted in favour of middlemen who are usually opposed to the demands of the workers, would pass to the financially distinct trade union store. When it is remembered how large a percentage of a city population either are, or soon will be, trade union, it will be seen what enormous power would thus pass to the workers. For the employers for the most part depend on what the poor buy, though they give the poor little wherewith to buy. The worker would, in strike or in work, have created the basis of his commonwealth, and the employer would find the enemy, who had thrown an army around his flank, encamped within striking distance of his sources of supply. Then the worker would proceed with caution and circumspection. He would choose what industry he would create for a beginning; choose with great care; throw his full weight into it (and trade union finances these days run into heavy moneys); find capable men, and pay them well; bring the latest science to bear on production; employ, especially in foodstuffs, the best of hygiene; and generally strive for the completest efficiency, while at the same time, even as the individual co-operative stores were pledged to buy from the Co-operative Wholesale, so the Co-operative Wholesale would discriminate always in favour of the Co-operative Manufacture. Indeed, such pledges would not be necessary, though they would be advisable, inasmuch as each higher organization being created by the funds of the lower it would be financially necessary for the lower organizations fully to support the higher in protection of their own funds. And thus finally a self-existent wide organization would evolve that would belong to the guilds of workers in commonwealth. Indeed, it is not too much to say that if in the early days of trade unions this policy had been adopted, the workers' battle would by now have been won and the commonwealth be partly now in existence, a civilization being thus created that would "provide for essential freedom for the individual and for solidarity of the nation" instead of weaving difficulties that now tend to disrupt the nationality and frustrate its State. "Men will gladly labour if they feel that their labour conspires with that of all other workers for the general good; but there is something loathsome for the spirit in the condition of the labour market, where labour is regarded as a commodity to be bought and sold like soap and candles." So says Æ, conceiving of a State as something other than a mere constitution; and history attests the truth of what he says, for men will sacrifice themselves for their State, whereas they regard a constitution as something separate from themselves.

Regarded from the point of view of labour, this state of affairs might be regarded as victory, victory won by organization instead of long warfare; and Æ is concerned for labour, being concerned for the dignity of man. Regarded from the point of view of the State it might be regarded as success, when the present system of exploitation, phrased as competition, is a pitiful failure; and Æ being concerned for Beauty and its implications and its concomitants, is concerned for the State. Yet the State itself does not emerge till all sides of the national life are co-ordinated; or, since a State is rather an expression than a device, it would be juster to say until all sides should co-ordinate themselves. And to this Æ turns. Already, it is worthy of remark, the problem has half answered itself. Even before the co-operative stores had created guild factories in cities in favour of which to discriminate, certain co-operative manufactures exist in favour of which discrimination could begin. These are the farmers' organizations, who are looking for markets, especially markets that would enable them directly to reach the consumer and in which they could become partners. With the very creation of co-operative stores for the cities, co-ordination, organized and economic, would begin. It would be for the interest of the farmers' guilds to promote such stores, and to exchange share holdings with them; and in truth one wonders why this has not already been done, since it is to the farmers' interest to banish the last of the middlemen and directly approach the consumer. So when, for instance, it came to the manufacture of farming implements, and indeed anything required for home or farm by the farmer, he could join with workmen's guilds in creating factories for the production of such things, and banish the last of the middlemen on the other side. The Commonwealth would then exist in completion, and the State emerge. The chief hindrance to so obvious a step is a certain prejudice based on ignorance. It faced Æ sharply when he saw how the farmers turned against the Dublin strikers; and so, with both sides of the false opposition claiming his sympathy, he faced the issue in an address at the annual meeting of the I.A.O.S.

His address was to farmers. How should they, in their own interests, wish to see town life develop? The articles which they, with help of Earth, manufactured, were not manufactured for the few and elect of the earth, not for the wealthy and privileged, but for all; they were indispensable if all were to live. Clearly, then, the more people who could afford to purchase them in sufficient quantities (seeing that men cannot eat more than a certain amount) the more they would be advantaged. Nay, more: rich men, having little manual toil, are fastidious of appetite, whereas working men are simple of taste and robust of appetite. If every man could afford to get for himself and his family as much food as they required, the spending power of the towns would at once be enormously increased to the direct benefit of the farmer, and every penny of that extra spending power would come from the poor, those who are continually striking in cities and towns for that extra food. "If there is, let us say," Æ says, "a sum of fifteen hundred pounds a week to be paid away in a town, it is to the interest of farmers that that sum should be paid to a thousand men at the rate of thirty shillings a week rather than to fifty men at thirty pounds a week. In the case of the workers, a greater part of the money will be spent on food. But if fifty men have thirty pounds a week each it will be spent to satisfy the appetites of a much smaller number of people. A larger proportion will be spent on furniture, pictures, motorcars, and what not. It may be spent so as to give some kind of employment, but it will not be a division of money so much to the interest of the farmer." So also should the farmer help the worker to eliminate the middlemen who stand betwixt them, for the cheaper food is the more freely will money be spent on it. Either way the farmer should support the worker's demands and his organizations in his own ripening interests.

Equally should the worker support the farmer of his own country in preference to the farmers of other countries. If he fail to support his own countrymen or if he give an equal welcome to produce coming from the four quarters of the world, the result will be that the home agriculturist will find the struggle hard against him, and will stream into the towns to produce blackleg labour: thus to cheapen his own wages, and thus, by depleting the agricultural army, to raise the cost of food against himself. Furthermore, by impoverishing his country he impoverishes himself. If a sack of oats be worth, say, a pound, every sack of oats grown in the country increases the financial reserve of that country by that pound. Men think too much in terms of the currency by the aid of which goods are bartered and not enough in terms of the goods, of which foodstuffs are the base, that are the real wealth. The present great war has provided an instance that Æ, and others besides, little considered at that time. Germany conserves her gold reserves by making a food-creating entity of herself, whereas England is continually depleting her gold reserves by despatching bullion overseas for the purchase of food; and so England, though she started infinitely the richer country, is rapidly approaching bankruptcy. Her industrial workers little dream what that will mean for the future. So also her merchant tonnage is being steadily reduced by submarine warfare and the need for troop transports, to an extent that few consider, so that foodstuffs cannot come to the country in the bulk that was once available. Thus, always, it is to the interest of the town-worker to support the farmer of his own country, even as it is to the interest of that farmer to support the demands of that worker for economic security. Each is a producer of something that the other cannot produce, and needs; each thus is a purchaser of the other's commodity; and it is to their mutual interests to see that they directly approach each other without the intermediary of profiteers, each producer taking, and being incited to take, an interest in the stores created by the other, and both by binding themselves together thus building up a State of Commonwealth.

So the economist displays his vigorous sense; so the poet shrewdly justifies his visions that are challenged, and finds a scope for their realization in a life of which he has experience. Ideals are always justified of Life, though some poets have avoided that challenge; and the poet here elaborates a State, every step of which is possible, many steps of which have been taken, many other steps of which are even now defining themselves for the future. It is a State that is democratic in the business of living, and it leaves freer play for the aristocracy of thought and emotion by withdrawing the individual from the absorption of money-grabbing. It makes a space for the fine flowers of divinity that will not blossom on the present soil, where titles of nobility are bestowed on men who have spent their lives brutal-izing themselves and others. It invites those flowers, indeed. When a rural community exists as a tribe, decreeing for the whole of its functions within its prescribed area, it will have to provide hedgerows and halls from its profits, and those hedgerows will be fruit-trees and those halls will demand architecture without and beautification within. The differ-ence will be small to each member when allotted out of the total available funds; and when one community has begun to aspire towards those flowers, the spirit of emulation will stir other communities. The poet, the musician, the painter, the architect, and the historian will have their honoured part in the life of the community as the possessions of that community, and will be matched against the like possessions in other communities. They would be attached to the court of the elected head of that community, the president of its deliberations; and the community would find it worth its while to endow them, that their making of beauty should be to the honour of itself, instead of compelling them to huckster their wares in a sordid competition of cash from which it had rescued itself. It is no dream, this. The spirit of it is not dead in Ireland. Even now, in a tradition dating from ancient times, little local poets "live on the commu-nity," and the people are content that they should do so. In a saner scheme of life they would have an allotted place; and the intellectual life of rural places, near the bosom of Earth, would not only vie with, but, drawing from simpler, from purer, from grander sources, would outrival the intellectual life of cities; and that which the world now so grievously needs, a new inspiration in Art, that has worn its old manner to shreds, would come of a new inspiration in Life and of larger experiences to canvas.

For what is this that the poet, pitting himself to find a hard economic answer for hard economic facts and not looking outside his immediate problem, has struck upon? It is even startling to conceive. It is nothing less than a translation into modern conditions of the ancient Polity of Ireland. The State for which we work in the future in answer to the problems of the present is the State that dwelt in our past. It is a conception of civilization that is our peculiar heritage; and it waits till it can come into our minds not as a patriot's dream (though all of this, and finely this), but as the unriddling of the tangle of Life into which we have got ourselves. When taunted once as not being at heart or by lineage an Irishman, he wrote a poem "On Behalf of Some Irishmen Not Followers of Tradition."

> They call us aliens, we are told,
> Because our wayward visions stray
> From that dim banner they unfold,
> The dreams of worn-out yesterday.

So he sings; and "flings his answer back in scorn":

> We are less children of this clime
> Than of some nation yet unborn
> Or empire in the womb of time.
> We hold the Ireland in the heart
> More than the land our eyes have seen,

> And love the goal for which we start
> More than the tale of what has been.

He turns from the "life men lived before":

> We leave the easy peace it brings:
> The few we are shall still unite
> In fealty to unseen kings
> Or unimaginable light.
> We would no Irish sign efface,
> But yet our lips would gladlier hail
> The firstborn of the Coming Race
> Than the last splendour of the Gael.

Yet he who sang thus thought more as a Gael than all the tribe of those who taunted him. He looked in his soul, and found ideals that have slumbered in our race through long oppression and repression: they looked at the foe against whose dominion they fought, and became bewitched by his ideals, wishing to plant another form of that alien thing in this country. Each became like the thing they steadfastly contemplated, in love or in hate; for it is the infallible rule of the soul that men become like the thing upon which they meditate.

Æ even worked in the Irish way. The *Feineacas* or Brehon laws, which image for us the old Irish State, have never received the attention they deserve; and there is a political reason for that. They have even been edited with misconceiving and belittling introductions from an English point of view, and with translations altered from those made by

the far finer Irish scholars, O'Donovan and O'Curry. The
Napoleonic Code, the Roman Code, even the far-removed
Hammurabi Code, have not failed of adequate exposition,
whereas the *Feineacas* have not yet taken their place in
international comparison, though they challenge comparison with any in a noble conception of Life. Yet how did
they come to be? Those other laws were, as all other laws
have been, abstractly conceived in legislative assembly or
princely edict; and abstractly codified; yet in none of them
is there an arresting ideal of Life. They are just workaday
administrative instruments, all that a lawyer would desire,
though, being abstractly conceived, there was both time
and opportunity to introduce into them some higher ideal.
The *Feineacas*, on the other hand, are just a medley of *ad hoc*
adjudications, the rough gathering together of judgments
given by brehons in their function as civil arbitrators, hard
to disentangle in their lack of systematic form. Yet what is
the result? Arising as they do from the clash of life in its
least savoury aspects, emerging as they do from disputes and
wrangles and their settlements, they yet display a conception of Life that arrests the mind with its dignity, humanity, and decency. Even so is it with the re-emergence of
this ancient Polity after long years in Irish life. John Stuart
Mill sat in his study and schemed a system of Economics.
Coming from that aloof and scholarly retirement it would
have been excusable had it worn a beauty too fair and
too virginal for the shock of Life. But it came calling itself
Utilitarianism, and was one of the intellectual lathers of a
scheme of Life that the world is beginning now to revolt
from as a sordid cynicism. Æ, and his comrades in work,

went out to a rough experience, to handle tough financial facts, to make a workable business organization, to think of pigs, cows, and poultry, living and dead, milk and eggs, manures and seeds, and to adjudicate in farming matters; and a system of Economics emerged with an arresting ideal of Life, dignified, humane, and decent, and with a hope for the future of humanity. It is not for nothing that the old Irish Polity is re-incarnated in the same experience as that in which it first was born — an experience, not only direct from the hard problems of life and their settlement, but from a farming life at that.

It is very strange to watch, and to participate in this emergence, of a distinctive and intensive Irish civilization, for it has been so long forgotten, even by the heroes of the nation. Ireland has fought long against England, with no other hope than to make another England of Ireland. That is only to break a political union to make a union of ideals; and that again is to abrogate nationality while espousing its cause. It is a hard thing to say, but true notwithstanding, that many of our later heroes have stood for nothing more than this. The splendid audacity of Wolfe Tone, simple and fearless and exuberant as that of a great child, the gentle nobility of Emmet, the forensic passion of Curran, the turgid eloquence of O'Connell, the pompous ineffectuality of Butt, dimmed by the clean hard mind that came after him — what distinctive Irish State did all this seek to achieve? Can any say? They opposed England with Ireland, which was fine; but they did not oppose English civilization with Irish civilization, and that is a great difference. There were only two minds that showed an understanding of the difference; and it is curious that both of them should have been charged (very falsely, let us say) with an alien characteristic. The scholarly Davis had glimpses of it in some of his essays; and there are implications in some of Parnell's speeches, dealing severely with tactical issues as they did, that seem as though he had some understanding of the difference. And what was Grattan's Parliament but a thing of the English Pale, with a vast and inarticulate Irish thought in the country, deliberately submerged, never permitted to raise its head? Grattan, though he acclaimed Ireland as "free" because she had won an abortive Parliament, was afraid of the Irish people as "people," Charlemont at the head of the Volunteers was afraid of the Irish people as "Catholics," and Flood was afraid of them as "Irish," standing as he did for ascendancy. Ireland may in her tragic history look back upon that Parliament within her own shores with some wistfulness, but the plain truth is this, that it was an alien thing, hostile to, and in craven fear of, the Irish Ireland that waited outside its doors.

It was left to this latter time to evolve, outside of Parliament, and despite the bitter opposition of Irishmen whose minds are subdued to English thinking, a distinctive Irish polity, the *Feineacas* beginning to be re-born in modern conditions, to construct an Irish State out of the practical experience of life, and to oppose English civilization, that is already self-condemned, with a distinctive Irish conception of civilization that has some hope for the future of Irishmen. And it is to Æ that the praise of this is due more than to any other. For what are his Rural Communities? They are neither more nor less than a reconstitution of the *tuatha*, the economic, social and political units of the old "tribal" organization of Ireland. "We have not had a social order since the time of the clans,"[9] he says in "Co-operation and Nationality"; and he is right; but that is due to no fault of ours, but due to those who feared lest we should put their own professed faith for the rights of small nationalities into good effect upon our own behalf. In "The Rural Community" he says: "We had true rural communities in ancient Ireland, though the organization was rather military than economic"; but there he is wrong. The *tuath* was hardly even military in a second-ary sense, and certainly it was not so primarily. From early times a certain order of *tuath* could claim the complete subordination of military duties to their economic life: they could not be called away at spring or at Harvest, and if at other times a provincial hosting should last for more than six weeks, at the end of that six weeks they had liberty to return home.[10] Therefore the *Fianna* were raised as a national militia from the older Firbolgs and Cruithni, or Picts, and were part of the army with which the great Niall harassed and defeated the Roman power through Britain and into Gaul. Cuchulainn, the "little dark man" and lord of the marches to Conchobhar, was such a man. When later they were suppressed for political reasons, it was the very economic preoccupation of the *tuatha* that made them the prey of the Normans, who were professional marauders without any economic life. And as the economic life of the *tuatha* still restricted their military power, foreign soldiers (*gall-ogláigh*, englished into galloglass, means foreign soldier) were imported and settled on the land by the consent of the *tuatha* to relieve them of the continual fighting to which they were compelled by the presence of this professional marauder. These *gall-ogláigh* came from the Hebrides, and were thus descended from the Irish conquest of the Isles mixing with the earlier and later Norse; but their introduction proves how intense was the economic preoccupation of these old rural communities; and proves also how the life of their modern counterpart reflects the life of their national original.

Each of these older communities was a recognized political unit, over which all conquest flowed, but indivisible because of the high social and economic organization it possessed; and towards this social and economic organization its modern counterpart is inevitably drifting, though clearer knowledge would shape that course better and effect it with less waste of experiment. The intuitions of a nation are not lost, though they be deliberately repressed; and what those intuitions first achieved as a conceivably fair civilization they will achieve again, though with the differences attendant on the different conditions affecting the accidentals of life. For those intuitions are nationality; and without them nationality is but a windy word. If wise statesmanship were to act from such intuitions, looking within at the continuing mind of its own nation instead of looking without at the mind of other nations, and give a political place to such economic and social units — political, that is to say, in the sense of being a unit in the Polity or State of the Nation — the conditions would repeat themselves even as in the past, and the State of the past would simply and automatically repeat itself in the future without the modern confusion of a continuing series of legislative instruments, none of which fit the complex need they seek to remedy, most of which are amended out of all recognition in practice, many of which are quietly dropped out of memory with nothing to remain of them but the pompous frivolity of their debate. And such a continuance would approve Nationality as a lasting fact, and not leave it as a protestation right or wrong.

For the conditions are the same. They are embedded, not only in national intuitions, but in the plain requirements of the case. The modern community needs a centre, a place where its necessary business may be conducted, its officers elected, around which its factories and creameries, its smithies and attendant crafts and industries, should be situated, and where it should engage in its recreations and its social pleasures, where lectures would be delivered, not only on matters arising out of its economic business, but also on wider national subjects, where those national issues might be debated, where, in the anticipations that our hope, faith, and love have prompted, the communal historian might discourse, the communal poet sing, the communal musician stir to emulation, and which the artist might design and beautify; and where, in a development happily native to our race, the community might extend its hospitality to strangers with dignity and good manners. The old community had such a need; and met it. The centre of its activities, social, economic, and public, was a building called the *Bruighin*, presided over by one who was called a *Bruigh-fer* or *Biadhtach*. It had land allotted to it by the *tuath* for its maintenance. Strangers received hospitality there. The two legislative and deliberative assemblies of the *tuath* met there to transact all business. The freemen of the *tuath* met there to elect their officers and to discuss public matters. Legal matters were settled there. And around it the craftsmen, artificers, and industrial workers lived, each with their separate guilds. The whole formed the capital township of the *tuath*. The *Bruighin* in no sense belonged to the *Bruigh-fer,* though he had his separate land, but was the joint property of the *tuath*. He was the officer of the community, dispensing its hospitality and calling its assemblies.

So if the communities rising now should wisely elect to endow artist and writer, it would have its example in the past. Such endowments are no necessary part of fantasy. Men in collective capacity acting together arise to public spirit as they are freed from personal competition. They esteem the dignities that give honour to life; and they esteem them the more if they can directly acknowledge them in small communities, and take honour by that direct acknowledgment, where a national acknowledgment by some public person, in which they have no hand, will leave them cold. That is human nature; even as it is human nature to care nothing for the honour and aspiration of Life when the whole business of living means a relentless and unremitting struggle of each man against all his fellows. Cleaner living means better leisure and higher dignity. Certainly, the modern community will need to pay, which is to endow, its chemists and scientists for its factories: were it not to do so, it would lose markets for its products. So it would need to endow its musician, as he would at once take his place in its dignities and its pleasures. Its *seanchaidhe* too, in the full meaning of the word, would soon find his place as lecturer. Since, therefore, the poet and the imaginative writer have an economic place in a community — that is to say, since their works must in some measure bring them profit — the community might well desire to absorb that economic place and yet find for the writer some security.[11] For it is not rash to assume that a life that depended on the application of individual thinking in large responsibilities would bring clean thinking in other matters than that of business. These things are no fantasy. The *tuath* did not find them so; but rather endowed its historian, its poets, and its musicians, even as it endowed its brehons and its public officers.

The *tuath*, however, was a complete economic entity. That is to say, it not only held land in community, not only did many of its members, as the *Crith Gablach* makes clear, hold farming implements in community, but it was its own source of self-help in all matters. It had its own local government; taxes, in modern phrase, being charged upon itself as a whole, for itself to recharge upon its members. Æ has spoken in "The Rural Community" of the modern co-operative community, electing to beautify its hedge-rows by planting fruit-trees, as has been done by some communities in Europe. Such things look forward to the rural community finding itself sole arbiter for its district, a community self-existent and indivisible, a political as well as an economic and social unit, relying on its self-aid and sufficient unto itself, though allying with others in larger federations and blending into a national conception. In that he looks back (though almost unwittingly) even as he looks forward: in desiring the Ireland that would answer his visions, and be based upon the answer experience has found for those visions, he sees "The Awakening of the Fires," for this is the Ireland of old born again. He sees not only a continuing Nation: he sees a continuing State, lying dormant a long while in dim intuitions but re-emerging at last in experience. It is strange how close the identity sometimes proves to be, and in ways of which he is unaware. For instance, while facing the whole of his rural problem he comes naturally to the case of the farm labourer. No State is fair, or worthy of all a man's effort, he says in effect, that bases itself on injustice in any of its parts. How is the problem of the farm labourer to be answered? The better prosperity of the farmer will in great measure help him; and the greater responsibility of farmers in a co-opera-tive society will help him, especially as he will inevitably form himself into a large union in the course of time. But then he throws out a suggestion. He says that labourers, while unable, individually to hold land, might profitably hold and work land in a company together, winning a dignity together that they could not severally compel. He does no more than leave it as a suggestion; yet it is straight from the ancient economy. In the *tuath* the lowest form of un-freeman was the *Fuidhir*. He was lower than the jack-boys and hirelings of the *tuath*, being generally a prisoner taken in war or an outlaw from some other tuath. Yet the *Feineacas* allowed him to join in some company of not less than five, to hold land together, and to appoint some one of their number to claim the rights of a freeman on behalf of the others if their several prosperity was consonant with the dignity, that consonancy being defined and decreed. The two things would in fact work themselves out to a close likeness, both being based on the land. And, indeed, it would not be difficult to speak of other developments towards which these co-operative societies of today are searching their way as they take their path towards becoming rural communities, in which they will find themselves like those who think they have broken into new country, who afterwards discover signs and ruins of the cities of their fathers who had lived here before them.

A man who preaches so completely the doctrine of self-help as the maker of muscle and thew in a nation, is not disposed to profess too loud a faith in parliamentarianism. In his eyes, parliaments have completed their function in the world. So long as they stood for a nation's general rights — the right to free thought, the right to free faith, the right to national action without the interference or prohibition of kingship — so long were they justified, so long had they their part to fill. But now that these things are in great measure fulfilled, the questions before parliaments have narrowed to those of particular rights: the right, for example, of the poor to economic freedom, to the control of the industries in which they are employed and which they by their labour build, the right to combine in order to effect these things. And here the poor always find that the jury is packed against them. In the liberties parliaments once achieved, the rich benefited with the poor; now the issues have narrowed against the rich, with the consequence that they have rallied together to capture parliaments, one company of them in one party nodding to another company in an opposite party with almost complete understanding. Nothing the poor can do can alter that fact. They must organize and work outside parliaments if they would win their freedom — which in truth is national freedom, for their overwhelming numbers make them the constituency of the nation. They must help themselves, for none other will help them; and in co-operation is the clue to that self-help, whereas nearly every act of a parliament avowedly or hiddenly desires to harness them, or sometimes feed them, in the interests of the wealthy, as they themselves too bitterly know. That is to say, they must legislate for themselves by creating for themselves the conditions of life and labour, and they must subordinate legislatures to the life of a nation instead of waiting for legislatures to dictate to that life in the interests of a few. They must be their own statesmen by being statesmen in fact.

It is little to be wondered at that Æ should so shrewdly suspect parliaments. In his early days, he had had his fighting heart aroused by seeing a hero of his nation stand single-handed in the ford to hack and hew an ancient parliament till it fell misshapen from his sword. When Parnell went to Westminster, the English House of Commons had a certain dignity and pomp of debate; and it was the centre of admiring attention; but as he sat on its benches he divined a certain heart of humbug in this pomp. He saw Bright espouse the cause of freedom in noble periods while giving the poor over to a system that should enslave them as never before. He heard Gladstone torrentially denounce the keeping of political prisoners in Neapolitan prisons while preserving a national silence over the Irish political prisoners less excusably kept in English prisons. These things he saw, and other things moreover. Then he rose up out of silence. He became the best hated man in England and the hero of Ireland; but he gave as little heed to applause as to anger. With deadly coldness he judged where his sword-play should fall, and judged with what strength it should fall; and when he ceased from his work, though a conspiracy not yet unfolded had brought him low, the assembly that had come to him with pomp and prestige left his hand a more or less submissive registration machine that was content to endorse the decisions of a secret committee. It is not for Irishmen, therefore, to praise the fair health and manliness of a figure that one of themselves left so misshapen; and Æ does not praise it, because he knows the powers that control that secret committee by the support of its war-chest. Yet that does not mean that he consents to the manacles placed on one nation by another with brute-strength, or the occasional kindness done with the lofty mien of the conqueror. His thought is far otherwise. He sees a distinct nationality with its own conception of civilization; and he would house that nationality in a distinct State worthy of the praise of noble men.

CHAPTER V

BYE-PATHS; AND PATHS EMERGING

To inaugurate the new century W.B. Yeats brought George Moore to a sense of style, as Philip Skelton brought the sinner "to a sense of religion," "by long perseverance, by his awful lectures, and the divine aid." To celebrate that fact they wrote a play together, "Diarmid and Grania," and persuaded Frank Benson to produce it at the Gaiety Theatre, Dublin. It is unnecessary to give the details of that enterprise. They have been preserved with meticulous accuracy by George Moore, the careful historian of latter-day art in Ireland. Æ, however, went to see the production of "Diarmid and Grania," and came to the conclusion that if this was drama then drama was an exceedingly easy thing to do. When he reached home that night, he straightway wrote the first act of a play dealing with Deidre. Having thus proved to himself that the playwright's art was just the simple thing he had thought it to be, he put the thing away in a drawer, went to bed, and thought no more of the matter. Yet that lone act lying in a drawer was to provide an important link. For some years before this the brothers W.G. and Frank Fay had been working at dramatic matters in Dublin, and had trained an amateur company to correct the loud theatricality of acting on the professional stage. Through diversity and adversity of experience, presenting plays in little halls where neither place, play, nor audience stirred the imagination, they yet kept before them the chance of finding a better scope for their effort. That chance came when they heard that Æ had become dramatist to the extent of one act of a play. Borrowing it, admiring it, and becoming ambitious of producing it, they persuaded Æ to finish the other two acts. This was very easily done. In the meantime W.B. Yeats had not forgotten his plays, some of which, including "The Countess Cathleen," had been produced the previous year with an English company in what was known as the Irish Literary Theatre: for a poet with a play to be produced is a lean and restless hunter in the world, a searcher with a swift eye for nobility in actors and still greater nobility in financiers. There were other such lean hunters. There was even a financier on the prowl with plays, one of the earlier company. Little wonder, then, that these fell together in a new dramatic fellowship. Æ, Edward Martyn, Padraic Colum, W.B. Yeats, Fred Ryan, Seumas O'Sullivan, and others, with Synge to join them rather later, and George Moore as embarrassing adviser, comprised that fellowship. The presidency was first offered to Æ, who declined it, as he felt that the writing of plays was not to be the highroad of his life, and suggested W.B. Yeats.

Later, when they were searching for more permanent headquarters at the Abbey Theatre, the feet of that presidency gave the leadership of the movement to W.B. Yeats, who associated with him J.M. Synge, and Lady Gregory who then joined the movement. There were other causes also Miss Horniman gave the movement money through Yeats, and under him it was formed into a Joint Stock Company, to the indignation of those who had made it what it was. Æ was too busy as co-operative organizer to write further plays, and thus fell away. George Moore turned again to thoughts of London. Edward Martyn had ecclesiastical doubts. The only playwrights of the original enterprise who remained with Yeats were Synge and Padraic Colum. The brothers Fay continued in control of the stage production. In the course of time, Padraic Colum's plays were no longer produced; and the brothers Fay also found it necessary to leave the company. Later historians have been too apt to judge of the beginnings of the movement by those whom they found in it at its latter end, when the earlier struggles had been won and the principles of acting learnt under masters who no longer appeared. It was Frank Fay, and no other man, who was responsible for the beautiful speaking of English and of verse, and for the just simplicity of gesture and position, that marked the acting of the company; and it was from him that Yeats received his ideas on these subjects. The fact that the Abbey Theatre afterwards reached a certain popular success by rejecting the ideals with which the confederacy began made that misconception easier, but it made it the more unjust. For those ideals, wherein it was sought to produce plays that were beautiful in a comrade-ship and co-operation as beautiful to match, remain the only possible way in which drama in Dublin will again become possible.

The moment from which events flowed was when Frank Fay, having heard of "Deidre," came to see Æ; and on April 2, 1902, "Deidre" was the first play to be produced, fol-lowed by W.B. Yeats' "Kathleen ni Houlihan." It attempted to be no more than a simple presentation of a tale of tragic beauty told in a prose as simple; but great tragedy comes not only from the tragic end of the tale that is told, but from some tragic weighting of it in the mind of the writer where it was received. The tragic poet is of the lineage of the prophets. He looks not only at his fable: his fable is only a medium through which he looks at the whole or a part of life. That is true also of the writer of comedy; and the distinction between tragedy and comedy, when each is at its best, is not so great in the end. In the loose and utterly foolish distinction raised by the tribe of critics between subjective and objective writing, it has been easily assumed that a lyric is subjective and the drama objective. What that means it is not easy to say. The truth is that a lyric may be easily disengaged from personality, springing up from some temporary mood, whereas a drama comes from the centre of an artist's conception of Life, it is coloured with the col-ours in which Life appears to him, it is weighted with the implications of all that seems for him involved in the issue of men together when they are charged with the deepest emotions. At its lowest, it hardens and crystallizes into the enunciation of a doctrine. At its highest, it is in that perfect solution from which many doctrines may be crystallized, and to which therefore philosophers turn as they would to Life itself, seeing some sharp vision of it through an intense mind. But always it is personality flowering in its bravest beauty; where the fable, and the casting of the fable, and the conflict of character through which the fable moves, and the manner of the solution into which it emerges and with which it suggests the untold thought, all utter to us a man's passionate vision of Life. And the height and depth of that vision, and the breadth and wisdom of it, becomes for us finally the clue by which we discover the greatness of the dramatist.

It is just this loading of the fable that we miss in "Deidre." It tells its tale — a pitiful tale that could be charged with so many significances — justly and truly as it came to Æ and in pure and musical prose. It does not express Æ to us: or rather, since it is impossible for a man to write without in some degree expressing himself, it merely carries off the things that had lightly gathered on the surface of his mind. The manner of its inception precluded a deep and meditated utterance; and leaves us with the thought that if Æ had not written with that marvellous facility of his, some of his later writings might more constantly have come burthened with permanent vision rather than radiant with a wonderful casual insight. In his essay on "The Dramatic Treatment of Heroic Literature," he contends against Standish O'Grady's protest that to serve the heroes of the past for pleasure on the stage is to degrade the ideals of the race. Later he came to something of Standish O'Grady's opinion; and at least believed that an adequate heroic drama was impossible. It seems worthwhile suggesting, more particularly in interpretation of "Deidre," that they both missed the essential matter. We are not interested in the deeds of the Red Branch as something that happened at some moment in the past: we are interested in those deeds in precisely the degree in which they happen in our minds today; and we are interested in the heroes that enacted them in the degree in which they are, or may by the intensity of the artist be made, qualities of our mind in the spiritual warfare in which we live, move, and have our being. If the dramatist can do this for us he will make the heroes great in the heroic thoughts that enrich our intellectual being; and that will only be because he has lived out their heroism in his measure in the familiar things of his own intellectual being. The world loses its heroes if it sees them in the past; but it gains them if it sees them in the perpetual present.

The dramatist who can do this will always be mocked with the intellectual sloth and derision of the many. That proves nothing. Or rather, it proves that that dramatist comes in good hour: it is a tribute, not to his inopportuneness, but to his punctuality. No true vision comes with peace, but with a sword. "Deidre," swiftly written for the brothers Fay to produce, did not bring that sword — and it was well, maybe, for the brothers Fay that this was so. At times, in sudden flashing lights, the play becomes charged with a further significance, as when Lavarcham (that significant figure in the old story) harps on the deep string that sounds the doom of Red Branch in the hour when Concobar should try to turn the natural flowing of the world to his own pleasure. But these lights when they flash up die away again, and the tale runs smoothly on again, to its ordered end. Though to demand highly of drama is right, especially when that demand is to be made of Æ, yet that demand in the case of "Deidre" will savour somewhat of churlishness, if not, indeed, of pedantry, for if the fable be not transformed and transfigured in its making it is at least purely formed and figured; and that is as much as he intended us to ask of it.

For he was putting his vision into other things. About that time he had returned to Dublin from organizing in the West, and occupied the position of Assistant-Secretary to the I.A.O.S. Living and married in Dublin, the painter's brush inevitably came into his hand again. When he had been in Dublin before, he had painted some of the visions he saw in the spiritual experience of the "household," illustrating both his poetry and his prose with the visions of the things that had prompted their writing. Now, however, he turned to a more systematic attempt to put in colour what in his experience he had seen so clearly; and to deepen that vision by recording as vision some of the deepest intuitions that had been stirred by his reading of the prophetic books of the world. These paintings were nearly all mystical, for he worked, assiduously enough and with increasing absorption, yet for his own enlightenment and pleasure, making gifts of his paintings to his friends, never thinking of a public display of them. But Count Markiewicz, who came to Ireland about that time, met him, saw his paintings, and, liking them, persuaded Æ to join him in an exhibition. There others also liked them; and exhibition followed exhibition through the years.

So, with time, a wider outlook began to mark his work. Though it be true that the mental decision with which Æ turned from mystical painting to the painting of landscape was prompted by the thought that he could better express mystical vision by poems, yet the true causes are deeper. The thought that prompts a decision is generally with men the first emergence of the decision from the hidden causes involved in many things: it is not in itself a cause but the first beginning of the actual result. When Æ resolved to turn to landscape painting, that result had already been decreed by the wider and more public conception of himself as an artist. A certain quality of his mind has divided him more sharply than with most into two men: the man who chooses things fit for public display before he displays them publicly, and the man who guards his esoteric things carefully from public curiosity. The two things do not often merge in Æ. It is not difficult, therefore, to see how he would shrink from letting a casual public pry into the hidden chambers of his life, with curiosity at best, and maybe with derision. Besides that, with the coming of the public it was inevitable that the artist should with the passage of time include a larger as well as a more immediate range of subject, that thus a greater scope should keep pace with the increasing maturity of touch and conviction of experience. And so he sought in the rhythms of figure and landscape for the beauty he had at first seen in psychic vision.

In his earlier pictures it is not the qualities of composition, symphony, and brush-work that chiefly arrest the
eye, although intensity of interest — indeed, sometimes in
his case an unworldly absorption of interest — includes
all the qualities of craftsmanship with the readiness with
which intuition, reaching forward to certitude of vision,
subordinates all means, even the least familiar, to its shining ends. Such qualities are always incidental to any artist
who is other than a technician, to be sure; and they are
the essential magic of art, whereby the artist becomes the
great spiritual discoverer as the things that seem incommu-
nicable begin to glow wonderfully in his own technique;
but in Æ's early work they are, we may say, peculiarly incidental. A fellow-craftsman may admire the composition
with which he blends some great figures of the Sidhe in
a slant perspective, a perspective that balances itself with a
suggestion of what does not appear, like a gesture outside
the canvas; or he may praise the ornamental skill with
which two figures in radiant glory are utilized to fill the
canvas without being themselves defined; but though an
artist secretly covets the approbation of his fellows, he does
not often address his canvases to them. We feel in these
paintings that the artist was in labour to communicate a
part of his assurance with regard to the spiritual beings
in the midst of which we are set, of the spiritual beings
we ourselves truly are; however fantastic his designs may
at first sight seem to us, that certitude of ours is the first
thing we have; and the result is that we hear the voice of
the critical exponent or analyst like a vague murmur in
our ears while we bend our minds to search into things

that become incomparably more than the artist and his art. Blake, who also painted mystical pictures, leaves us with this impression even less than Æ, because Blake, though a mystic, is more wholeheartedly an artist and Æ, though an artist, is in these early pictures we are at present considering, more wholeheartedly a mystic. In colour, for instance, Blake's colours are ordered by the symphonic value of the whole result, whereas it seems to us that Æ's colours, even while achieving it may be a gorgeous or very pure symphony of colour, are marked by a very earnest attempt at fidelity to psychic vision. They are both artists; but, while not wishing to be misunderstood, we may say that many of Æ's early pictures may almost by adepts be accepted as mystical charts, because these pictures are directly related to his mystical experience. Looking at them we begin to understand that when old warriors decked themselves with helmets or feathers suggesting plumes of light above the spinal cord, or wings branching from the temples, they were not merely fanciful; we remember that they lived in a day when vision and the psychic powers were not slighted in the world. So it is with line. Blake's rhythms, as for instance in the flames of hell that whirl a multitude of dead lovers while displaying Paolo and Francesca to us, Æ was afterwards to attempt in a different conception of his art; but in his early paintings his lines have another kind of fidelity altogether. It is different, naturally, with composition. Some of the best of his composition is seen when he seeks to bring within his canvas, in whole or in part, some very large design, and to suggest by his device what cannot be included.

This may seem to fall foul of his contention in the lecture on "Art and Literature" he delivered in the Royal Hibernian Academy to open a Watts Exhibition. There he protests against literary men who attempt to harness the artist with a formula of art; the Ruskins and Tolstois who would make artists subserve some ethical preconception of their own. It is worthy of remark that it is not only the artist in colour who has to endure wanderers from the pulpit: poets also have to exercise some sufferance; but the question is much deeper than that. Watts might paint some picture because he wished to impress us with some ethical sermon on Love and Life, and we might take some delight in his figures as things seen by the artist without at all knowing or at all caring which was meant to be Life and which Love; but when Æ paints some mystical picture, and we stand in gaze before it, seeing something more in it than its deftness or device of technique (which we afterwards recall), it is not because we have in our mind some ready literary doctrine of an ulterior purpose in Art. Not at all. And yet there is an ulterior purpose in Art; or it may be said, in a rapid paradox, that Art is itself that ulterior purpose. The artist says Æ justly and truly, painted his pictures because he delighted in what he saw. True; but that is not all, or very rarely is it all. For the artist paints his pictures also because he wishes us to delight in, or be awed by, what he saw. The whole of his composition is ordained to that end; and that fact gives it not the least of its definitions. From the point of view of the artist, his art is a series of momentous decisions for himself; but these decisions are momentous also because each of them is a communication. Among the many things that delighted him the artist chooses one to pass to others. That very choice implies an ulterior purpose. And, assuming a competency of skill lying ready for use, the rank of the result will be the rank of that purpose. The deftest skill will not atone for an unworthy conception, whereas a blundering craft will not often obscure a noble intention. That is to put the case in its extremest form; and the Ruskins and Tolstois of this world are chiefly annoying because it is not easy to see where it is and how it is they have managed to make a thing that is right appear so grotesquely wrong.

It may, or may not, be an exaggeration to say that when Æ painted his early pictures he wished each of them to communicate some spiritual or psychic vision that he judged of high importance that we should perceive if we are to thrive as spiritual beings in a spiritual world. Yet that is in essence true. They are like nothing that has been in latter-day art: they date back to an earlier conception of art, before art became a creed to itself. He is not therefore a national artist as Jack Yeats is; or even as Paul Henry is, though the latter's art may seem only to be national in the sense that a fine and finished craftsmanship learned in Continental schools is engaged upon national scenes and typical figures. These three are possibly the outstanding figures working with the brush in Ireland today, for the great and venerable personality of Nathaniel Hone, perhaps the greatest artist Ireland has produced, may be conceived as resting in a finished work. Of the three Jack Yeats is the complete national figure, unthinkable save in terms of Ireland. His technique itself is national; it is national as statuary is when it is memorable; for though it might be said that the sculptor belongs to the Stone Age, and Epstein as wittily reply that he must then be a Troglodyte, yet when a nation exerts itself in artistic expression it does so most energetically by the sculptor or the architect. Jack Yeats' art has a national quality. Foolish people have said that he has no technique, whereas they only mean that they do not understand his astonishing technique. His technique gives a perfect expression of his vision; and that is all that technique is meant to do. If he, for instance, revises in his drawing the relative sizes of things as they appear to the eye, he yet convinces that he is just to the relative sizes as they appear to his mind; he is like Gaelic syntax, that does not lay down an arbitrary and artificial sequence of subject, predicate, and object, but simply and precisely takes these things in the order in which the mental emotion approaches them. So he transfigures Ireland with a wonderful loving humour, where Paul Henry sees intensely and arrests what he sees in a fine economy of colour.

Yet Æ the artist is also national, though chiefly in his earlier work. It is difficult to conceive of just those mystical pictures being done in any other country. He lost that when circumstances compelled him to a less intensive range of themes, and the influences of other artists sometimes trail across his work. For those influences to be kept away, especially in a world that is hoary with memories of Art, an artist must be intensive in his work; and circumstances have caused Æ to be extensive. Yet he carries his spiritual intention with him. In a grouping of subjects and rhythm of line he suggests the spiritual world of which the world of landscape is an appearance; and the spiritual world does shine out through the world of appearance by the design and the symphony of colour into which he has inveigled it deftly; for in such pictures we see, though not always infallibly, that the mystic has never failed to search for spiritual things, knowing that the spiritual never passes away where material things are in continual flow and change.

For Æ faces life from many sides. It is difficult to write of a man in the midst of his work, with the tilth of it yet to be garnered. It is difficult to write, with that personal honesty without which books become only a profitable trade, of a friend. It is most difficult — especially as these other difficulties are attendant — to write of a man whose intellectual curiosity is so wide just because his spiritual curiosity is so intense. His speed of thought, and the intellectual impatience that that inevitably brings, arise from just that combination in the man. Whatever gives him aid in his spiritual interest is welcomed — a Wordsworthian cadence slipping into his poetry from his extraordinary literary memory, or some influence of Millet in his painting, or whatever it may chance to be. Whatever fails from spiritual understanding, or does not seem to him at that moment to possess spiritual endeavour, is dropped aside at once; and if it persist in forcing itself upon his attention it is attacked in the name of the high things for which he stands, and attacked lustily. It may be that sometimes he does not serve life so well by that impatience; for there is always the chance with impatience that it comes from imperfect understanding. When, for instance, bodies were mustering and arming throughout the country in the name of national freedom Æ asked of them at once, and very rightly asked, for what spiritual idea in the country were they arming. It was a noble question; and the leaders of that mustering, dear men though they be, foiled in intellectual courage and nobility in not conceiving of the national consciousness for which they stood, and in not defining, at least tentatively, the forms in which it should be cast as a just expression of itself. Arms are only noble when they are taken in defence of a noble thing that bravely faces all its consequences with clean sincerity. That is true; and very splendidly true; and coming from one who had faced his spiritual conception of the nation and thought out its consequences fearlessly, it was a just reproof. But national freedom, even when carried to its extremest limit, is also a spiritual ideal, that has proved itself worthy of the espousal of the noblest in the world's history; and they who claim it for one nation, where their influence does not extend, while denying it to another, arouse the disgust of honest men.

Æ has praised Alexander Hamilton. It is right also to praise George Washington, who made his work possible, and who was an equally noble figure. It was not while the right to a State in America was denied that the thought was possible that should engage itself in building that State. Irishmen all over the world have proved themselves quite sufficient statesmen; in fact, as Æ well claims, they are proving that already in the business and economic discussions of the various Co-operative Societies and Federations. Indeed, the right to a State of Ireland is not denied because of a fear that if it were granted it would be bungled, but because of the far more deeply seated fear that it would not be bungled.

And that fear springs from something more nauseous even than cowardice. It is, within its limits, justified; for the work of Co-operation in Ireland, directly it begins to win results that will challenge their place in the world, will then at once arouse the national hostility that piecemeal and deliberately in the past killed every Irish industry by some foreign State enactment, if by that time that hostility has not been stripped of its power to do harm. To think otherwise is to read history like a sentimentalist: is to deny that like things produce like results, as the teaching of history is.

Yet, in feeling that a public impatience (however apparently justified) sometimes may undo Æ's own good work, it is not necessary to go outside his life to find a certain pleasing parallel. It was not because he had thought out a place in the National Polity for factory workers that he sprang, like the fine fighter he is, into the fray on behalf of the Dublin strikers. No; it was because his being "went up in a blaze," because he was fighting before he well knew where he was, because every man's hand was against him whom till that time of trial he would have credited with philanthropic intent, that he began to think out the case of those who had so injuriously been done-by. And that is the human way. To think on the history of Ireland is to be maddened and sickened, for no nation in the whole course of history, past or present, has received from another the brutalities that have been accorded to Ireland: brutalities that are approved and endorsed in any man's mind who shrinks from their fullest reparation, whatever that entail, as no glossing can obscure; and it should be significant to Æ that it was the cleanest and best blood in the country, as one who knows may testify, that snatched arms for their country's liberty, even though they had not thought out the State in which the Nationality for which they stood should be expressed. If they wanted a creed, though they lacked definition of a State, one of the noblest of Æ's writings, dealing with "Nationality and Imperialism," would have provided it for them: "Some, even those who are Celts, protest against our movements as forlorn hopes. Yet what does it matter whether every Celt perished in the land, so that our wills, inviolate to the last, make obeisance only to the light which God has set for guidance in our souls? Would not that be spiritual victory and the greatest success? What would be the success we are assured of if we lay aside our hopes? What could we have or what could we give to humanity if our mental integrity is broken? God gives no second gift to a nation if it flings aside its birthright. We cannot put on the ideals of another people as a garment. We cannot, with every higher instinct of our nature shocked and violated, express ourselves as lovers of the law that rules us. We would be slaves if we did. The incarnate Love came not with peace but a sword. It does not speak only with the Holy Breath, but has in its armoury death and the strong weapons of the other immortals. It is better to remain unbroken to the last, and I count it as noble to fight God's battles as to keep His peace...." Those are great and noble words. The man who wrote them belongs not to a social aristocracy, though a social aristocracy flatter him. He is of the people of Ireland, even as he conceives the State that shall do honour to their nationality.

Other things may also temporarily upset him. A great war that is no less than a toppling civilization has disturbed him as it was bound to do. Not only, however, has it disturbed him by the fact of its being, but no less in the manner of its conduct. He expressed this, and also expressed himself, in a sonnet entitled "Chivalry":

> I dreamed I saw that ancient Irish queen,
> Who, from her dun, as dawn had opened wide
> Saw the tall foemen rise on every side,
> And gazed with kindling eye upon the scene,
> And in delight cried, "Noble is their mien."
> "Most kingly are they," her own host replied,
> Praising the beauty, bravery and pride,
> As if the foe their very kin had been.
> And then I heard the innumerable hiss
> Of human adders, nation with poisonous breath
> Spitting at nation, as if the dragon rage
> Would claw the spirit; and I woke at this,
> Knowing the soul of man was sick to death
> And I was weeping in the Iron Age.

So, in the well-knit speechcraft of his later verse, he comes to the making of the sonnet; the honoured vehicle of such saying as distinct from singing; and it leads him to the conclusion of "Tragedy," so deep in its application to more things than one:

> Love, the magician, and the wizard Hate,
> Though one be like white fire, and one dark flame,

Bye-Paths; and Paths Emerging

Work the same miracle, and all are wrought
Into the image that they contemplate.
None ever hated in the world but came
To every baseness of the foe he fought.

Yet out of that shock of conflict he sees new things coming; he sees the two foes that merge in battle in ideas also merging, each bestowing upon the other the very qualities against which the other is contending. That is for him "The Spiritual Conflict," whereby in the world of ideas the loser may become the victor, even as by contending against the new French democracy in the last great war the democratic idea became implanted in each nation. So in the future, he says, linking this new vision to the older body of his thought, "the coming solidarity is the domination of the State." There are, he adds, certain reactions "within one being, humanity," and these "indicate eternal desires of the soul. They seem to urge on us the idea that there is a pleroma, or human fullness, in which the opposites may be reconciled, and that the divine event to which we are moving is a State in which there will be essential freedom combined with an organic unity."[12] The bearing of this on what he had conceived of the State of Ireland is obvious, and is an enrichment of that conception. The irony of this spiritual conflict as reflected in the vital earnestness of the material conflict hardly needs mention. Believing that "the Universe exists for the purposes of soul", he looks for those purposes, and so fortifies himself in the bewilderment of change, for the changes are only apparent, and the purposes continue. So for the moment he steadies himself till he recover his old certitude. Thus it is that nothing can better conclude a study that has to arrest itself at the height of Æ's powers than his own forward glance, which he entitles "Continuity."

> No sign is made while empires pass.
> The flowers and stars are still His care,
> The constellations hid in grass
> The golden miracles in air.

> Life in an instant will be rent
> When death is glittering blind and wild —
> The Heavenly Brooding is intent
> To that last instant on Its child.

> It breathes the glow in brain and heart.
> Life is made magical, until
> Body and spirit are apart,
> The Everlasting works Its will.

> In that wild orchid that your feet
> In their next falling shall destroy,
> Minute and passionate and sweet
> The Mighty Master holds His joy.

> Though the crushed jewels droop and fade,
> The Artist's labours will not cease,
> And of the ruins shall be made
> Some yet more lovely masterpiece.

Endnotes

1   It is worthy of record also that the editor of the journal printing this, cut away its sterner parts. Malignity on the one hand and a very timorous friendship on the other are very typical of the attitudes towards Ireland

2   The Internationalist, vol. I. p. 36.

3   Co-operative Agriculture: A Solution of the Land Question," by Edward Pares. 1870

4   *Gaimbin* is the Irish for usurer. It is sometimes written "gombeen," but why the Irish language should be less entitled than any other to have its own spelling honoured it is hard to say

5   "Co-operation and Nationality."

6   "The United Irishwomen" p. 6.

7   See "The United Irishwomen; Their Place, Work and

Ideals," by Horace Plunkett, Ellice Pilkington, and George Russell (Æ). Maunsell.

8 "The Rural Community."

9 Strictly it is inaccurate to speak so. The *clann* was a gathering within the *tuath* due to its elaboration. The *tuath* was the equivalent of the "rural community." Nor are right terms in this matter a mere pedantry. To speak of the *clann* instead of the *tuath* is to miss the economic and political character of an exceedingly well-organized unit.

10 See "The Tribes and Customs of Hy-Many," p. 67.

11 The writer of hard or unpalatable things would be in no worse case than he is at present. Yet this might even be mended. Was not Basle well pleased to have Nietzsche for a professor, though he either did not read him or was outraged by his opinions? For Nietzsche's works were discussed and debated in other countries; and there is something pleasing in owning a celebrity, though he be only a notoriety.

12 This was printed in the London *Times*, not in "Rebel" Irish journal